THE

New Serial Question Books

ON

THE HEROES OF THE BIBLE.

IN FOUR VOLUMES,

GRADUATED TO ALL AGES.

NO. I. FOR INFANT CLASSES. NO. II. FOR CHILDREN
NO. III. FOR YOUTH. NO. IV. FOR ADULTS.

Fourth Series....For Adults.

By RUFUS W. CLARK, D. D.

PUBLISHED FOR THE AUTHOR.

BOSTON:
FOR SALE BY MASS. S. S. SOCIETY, HENRY HOYT, GRAVES & YOUNG.
NEW YORK: M. W. DODD, A. D. F. RANDOLPH.
PHILADELPHIA: W. S. & A. MARTIEN.
ALBANY: S. R. GRAY, FISK & SON.

ABBREVIATIONS.—Besides the abbreviations of the books of the Bible, the following are used: f. c. first clause of a verse; m. c. middle clause; l. c. last clause. B. C. Before Christ. A. D. Year of our Lord. Comp. Compare.

PREFACE.

THIS volume is designed for adults, and may be studied with the aid of a Commentary, and a Bible Dictionary.

The questions, answers, and references given are designed simply to introduce the student to the study of the sacred characters and great historical facts of the Bible, with the hope that they may be thoroughly investigated, and that the important lessons which they teach may be deeply impressed upon the mind and the heart. The more intimately we become acquainted with these illustrious Heroes, the more distinctly we see the providence of God in their history, and the power of virtue and holiness to confer personal happiness and national prosperity. The Bible gives us not only the principles of religion, but the most vivid and impressive illustrations of its practical effects.

May all who study the lives and achievements of these holy men imbibe their spirit, possess their faith, and meet them at last in the heavenly Jerusalem, — the city of the living God!

INDEX.

QUESTIONS

ON THE

HEROES OF THE BIBLE.

Fourth Series.—For Adults.

LESSON I.

ADAM, THE FATHER OF THE HUMAN FAMILY.

1. Who is the great first Cause of all things?
2. What proof is there that mind existed before matter? Gen. i. 1; Ps. xxxiii. 6.
3. What is the meaning of the word "create"?
4. For what purpose were the heavens and the earth created? Rev. iv. 11.
5. How was Adam created? Gen. ii. 7.
6. How are man's two natures here distinguished as to their origin?
7. In whose image was Adam created? Gen. i. 27.
8. What can you say of his exalted nature? Ps viii. 5.
9. What rank did he hold? Gen. i. 26; Ps. viii 6–8.
10. What can you say of the value of the soul of man? Matt. xvi. 26.
11. What was the character of the preparations made for Adam? Gen. i. 31.
12. What is the character of the Being who made these preparations? Ps. c. 5; cxlv. 9.

13. What do the works of God declare? Ps. xix 1; Rom. i. 20; Ps. cxlv. 10.

14. Where was Adam first placed by the Almighty? Gen. ii. 8.

15. Why was he placed in the garden of Eden? Gen. ii. 15.

16. Where was this garden situated? *Ans.* It is impossible accurately to determine. Many writers have located it upon the elevated lands of Armenia. Others in Persia, near the spot where the Euphrates and Tigris form a junction.

17. To what moral test was Adam subjected? Gen. ii. 16, 17.

18. Had the Creator a right to issue this command? Gen. xviii. 25, l. c.; Deut. xxxii. 4; Ps. lxxxix. 14.

19. Was it best that Adam should be thus tried? James i. 12.

20. Did God tempt him to sin? James i. 13.

21. Was there anything in his nature to incline him to sin? Eccl. vii. 29.

22. How was he led to transgress the laws of God? Gen. iii. 4–6.

23. What was the penalty of disobedience? Gen. ii. 17, l. c.

24. What effect had a sense of guilt upon Adam and Eve? Gen. iii. 8–10.

25. What sentence was pronounced upon the serpent? Gen. iii. 14.

26. What did God say to the woman? Gen. iii. 16.

27. What sentence did he pronounce upon Adam? Gen. iii. 17–19.

28. What calamity followed the first sin? Gen. iii. 23, 24.

29. What promise was make to Adam? Gen. iii. 15.

30. Was this promise fulfilled? Heb. ii. 14.

31. What proof is there that mankind descended fr m one pair? Gen. iii. 20; 1 Cor. xv. xxii.

LESSON II.

ABEL, THE FIRST MARTYR.

1. What were the names of Adam's two oldest sons?
2. What does Cain signify? *Ans.* Possession.
3. What does Abel signify? *Ans.* Vanity.
4. What were their employments? Gen. iv. 2.
5. Why were they obliged to labor? Gen. iii. 19
6. What was the first religious institution established by God? Gen. ii. 2, 3.
7. Was it designed to be perpetual? Ex. xx. 8.
8. What proof is there that the Sabbath was early observed? Ex. xvi. 25, 26, 30; Lev. xxiv. 8.
9. What promises are made to those who keep the Sabbath? Is. lviii. 13, 14; lvi. 6, 7.
10. What other religious institution was early established? Gen. iv. 3; xxxi. 54.
11. What kind of offerings did the Lord require? Num. xviii. 12, 13.
12. What did Abel bring to God? Gen. iv. 4.
13. What was required in respect to the animals offered in sacrifice? Lev. xxii. 20–24.
14. How did God regard the offering of Abel? Gen. iv. 4, l. c.
15. In what manner might this regard have been expressed? Lev. ix. 4.
16. What principle must we exercise in coming to God? Heb. xi. 6.
17. Did Abel exhibit this? Heb. xi. 4, f. c.
18. What witness did he obtain? Heb. xi. 4, m. c
19. What offering did Cain bring to the Lord? Gen. iv. 3.
20. How was his offering regarded? Gen. iv. 5.

21. Why were Cain and his offering not regarded with respect? *Ans.* Because his offering was not accompanied with right feelings toward God, and was not, like Abel's, a sacrifice for sin.

22. How did God's disapprobation affect Cain? Gen. iv. 5, l. c.

23. Had he any just reason for being angry?

24. What appeal was made to him? Gen. iv. 6, 7.

25. What does this language imply in relation to his wrong-doing?

26. What was the character of Cain? 1 John iii. 12.

27. How did he show the wickedness of his heart? Gen. iv. 8.

28. Was Abel at all to blame for the failure of Cain to secure the approbation of God?

29. What evil principles in Cain prompted this murder?

30. By what statutes was the horrible nature of the crime of murder inculcated? Num. xxxv. 30–34; Deut. xxi. 1–9.

31. What inquiry did the Lord make of Cain after this sad event? Gen. iv. 9, f. c.

32. What reply did Cain make? Gen. iv. 9, m. c.

33. What additional sin did he commit?

34. What punishment was inflicted upon him? Gen. iv. 11, 12.

35. What sacrifices does God require? Ps. li. 17; Is. lvii. 15.

36. Why should Abel be regarded as the first martyr?

LESSON III.

ENOCH, THE HERO WHO WALKED WITH GOD.

1. How full is the account that we have of the patriarch Enoch?

2. Is it necessary to have all the details of a man's life to judge of his character and the importance of his position?

3. How many years after the creation of Adam was Enoch born? *Ans.* 622.

4. Who was the father of Enoch? Gen. v. 18.

5. How many years did Adam and Enoch live together upon the earth? *Ans.* 308.

6. How, at that period of the world, was a knowledge of the history of the creation and of religious institutions preserved?

7. How did Enoch obtain a knowledge of the true God, and of his religious obligations and duties?

8. Was parental instruction very early inculcated? Comp. Deut. vi. 7.

9. How is Enoch's religious character described? Gen. v. 22.

10. What other saints are spoken of as having "walked with God"? Gen. vi. 9; xxiv. 40; 2 Kings xx. 3.

11. What commands are obeyed by those who walk with God? Deut. vi. 5; x. 12.

12. What promises are made to those who love God? Rom. viii. 28; 1 Cor. ii. 9.

13. What feelings are entertained by those who walk with God? Ps. lxxiii. 25, 26; Is. xxvi. 9.

14. For what was Enoch distinguished besides his eminent piety? *Ans.* He is said, by an ancient author, to have been the father of astrology; and Euse-

bius advances the opinion that he is the same with the "Atlas" of the Grecian mythology.

15. Upon what better basis than this does his fame rest?

16. How was Enoch rewarded for his piety? Gen. v. 24.

17. What is meant by the words "God took him"? Heb. xi. 5.

18. Did his body, while being translated, probably undergo a change? Comp. 1 Cor. xv. 40, 44, 50.

19. What testimony did he receive before he was translated? Heb. xi. 5, l. c.

20. How did he probably receive this testimony?

21. How do we know when we please God? Eccl. ii. 26; Ps. v. 11, 12.

22. Can you mention another instance of translation to heaven? 2 Kings ii. 11.

23. Who was carried up into heaven after having conquered death and brought life and immortality to light? Luke xxiv. 51.

24. How many years did Enoch live upon the earth? Gen. v. 23.

25. What sacred office did he hold? Jude 14.

26. What prophecy did he utter? Jude 14, 15.

27. What do we learn from this of the moral state of the world at that period?

28. How can we secure the blessings that Enoch obtained? Jude 20, 21.

29. What will be our prospects for the future if we now walk with God? Rev. iii 4; 1 John iii 2; Rom ii. 7; Rev. vii. 15–17.

LESSON IV

NOAH, THE PREACHER OF RIGHTEOUSNESS.

1 Who was the father of Noah? Gen. v. 28.

2. Why did Lamech call his son Noah? Gen. v. 29

3. What was the moral state of mankind in the days of Noah? Gen. vi. 5.

4. How did God view the wickedness of man? Gen. vi. 6.

5. What is meant by the words "the Lord repented"? *Ans.* He changed in his dealings with his creatures, because they had changed toward him by sinning against him.

6. On what other occasion is the Lord said to have repented? 1 Sam. xv. 10, 11.

7. Does he repent in the sense in which man repents? Num. xxiii. 19; James i. 17.

8. On what principles does God deal with men? Deut. xxxii. 4; Ps. lxxxix. 14.

9. What purpose did the Lord form in relation to the wicked on the earth? Gen. vi. 7.

10. What was the character of Noah? Gen. vi. 9.

11. How wide-spread was the corruption around him? Gen. vi. 5.

12. What revelation did God make to Noah? Gen. vi. 13.

13. How many years before the flood was the event made known to Noah? Gen. vi. 3, l. c.

14. What directions were given to Noah in regard to building the ark? Gen. vi. 14–16.

15. What is the length of a cubit? *Ans.* One foot and a half.

16. Give the dimensions of the ark in feet.

17. What influenced Noah to build the ark? Heb. xi. 7.
18 How did Noah serve God? 2 Peter ii 5.
19. Did the people, under his preaching, prepare for the deluge? Matt. xxiv. 37, 38.
20. Why did they not prepare?
21. Of what great calamity are men now forewarned? 2 Peter iii. 10.
22. Are the great majority preparing for it?
23. How old was Noah when the deluge commenced? Gen. vii. 11.
24. Who were saved in the ark with Noah? Gen. vii. 13.
25. What living creatures were saved? Gen. vi. 19, 20.
26. How extensive was the deluge? Gen. vii. 18–20.
27. How extensive was the destruction of life? Gen. vii. 21–23.
28. What command came to Noah when the ground was dry? Gen. viii. 15, 17.
29. What act of piety did Noah perform when he left the ark? Gen. viii. 20.
30. What blessing did God pronounce upon Noah? Gen. ix. 1, 2.
31. What covenant was made with him? Gen. ix. 11.
32. What was the token of the covenant? Gen. ix. 12, 13.
33. What promises made to Noah have been fulfilled? Gen. viii. 21, 22.

LESSON V.

JOB, THE HERO OF PATIENCE.

1. Was Job a real person, or a fictitious character? Ezek. xiv. 14; James v. 11.

2. Where did he live? Job i. 1.

3. Where was the land of Uz? *Ans.* In Eastern Edom.

4. At what time did Job live? *Ans.* The precise period of his life cannot be ascertained. Some writers place him before Abraham, and others say that his trial occurred 1521 B. C.

5. What was the character of Job? Job i. 1.

6. For what particular virtue was he distinguished? James v. 11.

7. Give some account of his family and property. Job i. 2, 3.

8. What charge did Satan bring against him? Job i. 9–11.

9. What proofs can you give of the existence of evil spirits? Eph. vi. 12; Luke iv. 41.

10. What will be the result of resisting them? James iv. 7; Eph. vi. 16.

11. What did the Lord permit Satan to do? Job i. 12.

12. Give an account of the calamities that befell Job. Job i 13–19.

13. How was Job affected by these trials? Job i. 20, 21.

14. What enabled him thus to bear up against them?

15. How was he again severely tried? Job ii. 7, 8.

16. What bad advice did his wife give to him? Job ii. 9.

17. What reply did Job make? Job ii. 10.

18. How ought we to feel under afflictions? Job xiii. 15; Hab. iii. 17, 18.

19. Who came to comfort the sufferer? Job ii. 11.

20. How were they affected? Job ii. 12, 13.

21. How did Job express his sorrow? Job iii. 3–6.

22. What new assault is made upon him? Job iv. 7–9.

23. What good advice does Eliphaz give to Job? Job v. 8–11.

24. What advice does he give that is applicable to all? Job v. 17.

25. What divine attributes does Bildad unfold? Job viii. 3–6.

26. In what language does Job present the justice and power of God? Job ix. 4–10.

27. How does he present the shortness and vanity of human life? Job vii. 6, 9; ix. 25, 26.

28. What great truth does Zophar bring out in his speech to Job? Job xi. 7–9.

29. What exhortation does he make to Job? Job xi. 13–17.

30. What just reproof does Job give to his friends? Job xiii. 2–13.

31. How does he again describe human life? Job xiv. 1–12.

32. How does he express his great confidence in God? Job xix. 23–26.

33. How was he rewarded for his patience? Job xlii. 12, 13.

34. What important lesson may we learn from the dealings of divine Providence? 1 Peter ii. 20.

LESSON VI.

ABRAHAM, THE FRIEND OF GOD.

1. Where was Abraham born? *Ans.* At Ur, of the Chaldees, a city situated between Nineveh and Nisibis.

2. In what year of the world was he born? *Ans* 2009.

3. How long after the deluge? *Ans.* 350 years.

4. Whose son was Abraham? Gen. xi. 27.

5. How many generations was he from Adam? *Ans.* There were ten generations from the creation to the deluge, and ten from the deluge to Abraham.

6. What was the religious character of his family connections? Josh. xxiv. 2.

7. By what titles was he known? Rom. iv. 11; James ii. 23.

8. What was the religious condition of Chaldea at this time? *Ans.* At this period, and for a long time afterward, idolatry and superstition prevailed, and the people worshipped the sun, moon, and stars.

9. What command came to Abraham? Gen. xii. 1.

10. Why was he directed to leave his country and kindred?

11. What great promises were made to him? Gen. xii. 2, 3.

12. How old was Abraham when he departed out of Haran? Gen. xii. 4.

13. Who accompanied him out of Haran? Gen. xii. 5.

14. Give some account of the journey. Gen. xii. 6–9.

15. What is said of the wealth of Abraham? Gen. xiii. 2.

16 For what noble qualities was he distinguished? Gen. xiii. 8, 9; xiv. 22, 23.

17. What proof have we of his generous hospitality? Gen. xviii. 1–8.
18. How was he esteemed by others? Gen. xiv. 18–20.
19. What encouragement had he from his God? Gen. xii. 7; xv. 1.
20. What message came to him when he was ninety-and-nine years old? Gen. xvii. 1, 2.
21. What was included in the covenant made with Abraham? Gen. xvii. 4–6, 8.
22. How long was this covenant to stand? Gen. xvii. 7.
23. What was to be the token of the covenant? Gen. xvii. 9–14.
24. Did the covenant include spiritual as well as temporal benefits? Luke i. 72–75; Rom. iv. 16; v. 1, 2.
25. Upon what conditions can the spiritual blessings be obtained? Matt. iii. 8, 9; Rom. ii. 28, 29.
26. Was the promise "I will make of thee a great nation" fulfilled? 2 Chron. i. 9; 1 Kings iii. 8.
27. Did God make Abraham's "name great" in the earth? John viii. 53; Acts vii. 2; Rom. iv. 16.
28. How was the promise fulfilled, "In thee shall all families of the earth be blessed"? Gal. iii. 8–14; Heb. ii. 16, 17.
29. How may we obtain the rich blessings that come through Abraham? Gal. iii. 29.
30. What characteristics will mark the true seed of Abraham? John viii. 39.
31. Who will at last sit down with Abraham in the kingdom of heaven? Matt. viii. 11.
32. Who will be cast out? Matt. viii. 12.
33. Why will they be cast out? Matt. iii. 7, 10, xxiii. 13, 14.
34. What duty presses upon us? Luke xiii. 24.

LESSON VII.

ABRAHAM, THE HERO OF FAITH.

1. What blessing did God bestow upon Sarah, the wife of Abraham? Gen. xvii. 16.
2. How was Isaac connected with the covenant? Gen. xvii. 19.
3. What is the meaning of a covenant?
4. What is meant by a covenant of works? Gen. ii. 17; Is. i. 19, 20.
5. What is meant by the covenant of redemption? Ps. lxxxix. 3, 27–29; 2 Tim. i. 9.
6. Was the promise of God to Sarah fulfilled? Gen. xxi. 1, 2.
7. What command did Abraham obey in relation to his son? Gen. xxi. 4.
8. Why was Isaac circumcised?
9. How old was Abraham when his son Isaac was born? Gen. xxi. 5.
10. Why was Isaac particularly dear to his father? Gen. xvii. 21.
11. What evidence did Abraham give of his affection for his son? Gen. xxi. 8.
12. What is God said to have done to Abraham? Gen. xxii. 1.
13. In what sense was Abraham tempted?
14. Are there temptations, or trials, in which we may rejoice? James i. 2; 1 Peter i. 6.
15. What are some of the fruits of these trials? James i. 3; 1 Peter i. 7–9.
16. To what great trial was Abraham called? Gen. xxii. 2.
17. What is meant by the land of Moriah? *Ans.*

It is supposed to include all the mountains of Jerusalem.

18. How far distant was this locality from Beersheba, the residence of Abraham? *Ans.* About forty-two miles.

19. Did Abraham obey the command of God? Gen. xxii. 3.

20. How long did they travel before they reached the spot whither God directed them? Gen. xxii. 4.

21. Of whom was Isaac the type?

22. Who bore the wood for the sacrifice? Gen. xxii. 6.

23. Of what was this typical? John xix. 17.

24. What touching question did the son put to the father? Gen. xxii. 7.

25. What reply did the father make? Gen. xxii. 8.

26. Did God indeed long afterward provide a Lamb? John i. 29.

27. What preparations were made for the sacrifice? Gen. xxii. 9.

28. Was Isaac willing to be offered up?

29. Of what was this typical? Matt. xxvi. 39, 42.

30. Who stretched forth his hand to slay Isaac? Gen. xxii. 10.

31. Of what was this typical? John iii. 16.

32. What title is given to the son offered up by Abraham? Heb. xi. 17.

33. What title is applied to the Son given up by our heavenly Father? John iii. 16; 1 John iv. 9.

34. How was the knife arrested, and the life of Isaac saved? Gen. xxii. 11, 12.

35. Why was this trial sent upon Abraham? Gen. xxii. 12, l. c.; James ii. 22.

36. How did God provide a lamb for the sacrifice? Gen. xxii. 13.

37. What promises were made to Abraham, as a reward for his faith? Gen. xxii. 15–18.

LESSON VIII.

ISAAC, THE EXAMPLE OF PRIVATE VIRTUES.

1. In what year of the world was Isaac born? *Ans.* 2109.

2. Why did his father feel so deep an interest in him? Gen. xvii. 21.

3. What trial had he in his childhood? Gen. xxi. 9.

4. What was done to Hagar and her son? Gen. xxi. 14.

5. Did God provide for them? Gen. xxi. 17–21.

6. What explanation does St. Paul give of this matter? Gal. iv. 28, 29.

7. Was the conduct of Ishmael very offensive? Gen. xxi. 11.

8. What virtues did Isaac doubtless manifest when laid upon the wood for sacrifice?

9. Whom did he represent in this? Is. liii. 7.

10. How did Abraham, in his old age, manifest his anxiety for the domestic welfare of his son? Gen. xxiv. 1–4.

11. Why did he not wish Isaac to take a wife from the daughters of the Canaanites? Deut. vii. 3, 4.

12. How did Abraham show his entire confidence in God? Gen. xxiv. 7.

13. Did God direct his servants by an angel? Ex. xxiii. 20, 23; xxxiii. 2.

14. Whither did the servant of Abraham go? Gen. xxiv. 10.

15. Where did he rest? Gen. xxiv. 11.

16. What prayer did he offer up? Gen. xxiv. 12–14.

17. Was this prayer answered? Gen. xxiv. 15.

18. What did he say to the damsel? Gen. xxiv. 17.
19. How did she show her kindness? Gen. xxiv. 18–20.
20. How did she display her hospitality? Gen. xxiv. 25.
21. What effect had her conduct upon the servant of Abraham? Gen. xxiv. 26, 27.
22. Give an account of the interview between Isaac and Rebekah. Gen. xxiv. 63–67.
23. For what qualities and attractions was Rebekah distinguished?
24. What virtues were prominent in the history of Isaac?
25. What was the age of Isaac at the time of his marriage? Gen. xxv. 20.
26. What is said of his children? Gen. xxv. 27, 28.
27. What blessing was pronounced upon Isaac? Gen. xxvi. 2–4.
28. Why was this blessing pronounced upon him? Gen. xxvi. 5.
29. How was he favored in his worldly interests? Gen. xxvi. 12–14.
30. How did God regard him? Gen. xxvi. 24.
31. How did Isaac manifest his piety? Gen. xxvi. 25.
32. What should be the purposes of our hearts? Ps. cxvi. 17–19.

LESSON IX.

JACOB, THE FAVORED SON.

1. In what year of the world was Jacob born? *Ans.* 2169.

2. How long had his parents been married before his birth? *Ans.* 20 years.

3. How was this a trial of their faith?

4. What is the meaning of Jacob? *Ans.* The supplanter.

5. What important event brings Jacob conspicuously before us? Gen. xxv. 29–31.

6. Was it right for Jacob to take advantage of his brother's hunger and exhaustion?

7. Did Esau properly value his birthright? Gen. xxv. 32–34.

8. To whom did the birthright belong?

9. What privileges had the first-born son? Gen xlix. 3; 2 Chron. xxi. 3.

10. How does St. Paul view the character of Esau? Heb. xii. 16.

11. What revelation of God's purpose was made in regard to the two brothers? Gen. xxv. 23.

12. What were the feelings of the parents toward them? Gen. xxv. 28.

13. Upon whom did Isaac intend to bestow his blessing? Gen. xxvii. 1–4.

14. What plan did Rebekah lay to defeat the design of Isaac? Gen. xxvii. 5–10.

15. What further preparations were made? Gen. xxvii. 15–17.

16. How did Jacob deceive his father? Gen. xxvii. 18–23.

17. Is his conduct in this matter at all excusable?

18. What blessing was pronounced upon him. Gen. xxvii. 28, 29.

19. What divine purpose was brought to view in the words, "Let people serve thee"? Gen. xxv. 23, l. c.

20. With what other divine purposes was this blessing connected? Gen. xii. 2, 3.

21. What took place "as soon as Isaac had made an end of blessing Jacob"? Gen. xxvii. 30, 31.

22. How was Isaac affected when he discovered the deception that had been practised upon him? Gen. xxvii. 32, 33.

23. How was Esau affected? Gen. xxvii. 34.

24. How did the father answer his plea for a blessing? Gen. xxvii. 39, 40.

25. What principle actuated Isaac in pronouncing these blessings? Heb. xi. 20.

26. Why could he not revoke the prophetic words addressed to Jacob? 2 Peter i. 21.

27. Were the blessings bestowed upon Esau temporal or spiritual?

28. Who were the descendants of Esau? *Ans.* The Edomites.

29. Were their lands fruitful, according to the promise made to Esau? Num. xx. 17.

30. Were the other prophecies fulfilled? 2 Sam. viii. 14; 2 Kings viii. 20.

31. Were the promises made by Isaac to Jacob confirmed by God? Gen. xxxv. 9-12; 1 Chron. xvi. 17.

LESSON X.

JACOB, THE TRIED EXILE.

1. How did Esau feel toward Jacob? Gen. xxvii. 41, f. c.
2. What wicked purpose did he form in his heart? Gen. xxvii. 41, l. c.
3. What plan was formed to save the life of Jacob? Gen. xxvii. 42–45.
4. What charge was given to Jacob, on leaving his father? Gen. xxviii. 1, 2.
5. What proof is given that Isaac was convinced that he was fulfilling the divine will in blessing Jacob? Gen. xxviii. 3, 4.
6. Whither did Jacob go? Gen. xxviii. 10, 11.
7. What occurred to him while sleeping? Gen. xxviii. 12.
8. What did the Lord say to him? Gen. xxviii 13–15.
9. Was the prophecy in regard to his seed fulfilled? Num. xxiii. 10.
10. What impression did this scene make upon his mind? Gen. xxviii. 16, 17.
11. How did he show his piety toward God? Gen. xxviii. 18.
12. What did the pouring on of the oil indicate? Lev. viii. 10, 11, 12; Num. vii. 1.
13. What did Jacob call the place? Gen. xxviii. 19.
14. What is the meaning of Bethel? *Ans.* The house of God.
15. What vow did Jacob make? Gen. xxviii. 20–22.
16. Who, before him, had given a tenth to the Lord? Gen. xiv. 20.

17. Did the giving of tithes become a law? Lev. xxvii. 30.

18. Give an account of Jacob's meeting with Rachel. Gen. xxix. 9–12.

19. How did Laban receive him? Gen. xxix. 13, 14.

20. What arrangement was made between them in regard to Rachel? Gen. xxix. 16, 18.

21. As Jacob had deceived his father, how was he now deceived? Gen. xxix. 23.

22. After serving seven years for Rachel, what other trials befell him? Gen. xxix. 27; xxxi. 7.

23. What command came to him from God? Gen. xxxi. 13.

24. Did Jacob obey? Gen. xxxi. 17, 18.

25. How long had he been with Laban? Gen. xxxi. 41.

26. Who sustained him through his trials? Gen. xxxi. 42.

27. What proposition did Laban make to Jacob? Gen. xxxi. 44.

28. Did Jacob assent to it? Gen. xxxi. 45, 46.

29. What did Laban call the heap of stones? Gen. xxxi. 47, f. c.

30. What is the meaning of Jegar-sahadutha? *Ans.* The heap of witness. Chaldee.

31. What did Jacob call it? Gen. xxxi. 47, l. c.

32. What is meant by Galeed? *Ans.* It is a Hebrew word, and signifies "The heap of witness."

33. What other name was given to it? Gen. xxxi. 49.

34. What is the meaning of Mizpah? *Ans.* A beacon or watchtower.

35. Of what was this heap the pledge? Gen. xxxi. 52.

36. What pious act did Jacob perform? Gen. xxxi. 54.

37. How did they separate? Gen. xxxi. 55.

LESSON XI.

JACOB.—THE FRATERNAL MEETING.

1. As Jacob went on his way, who met him? Gen. xxxii. 1.
2. Are angels sent forth to aid the servants of God? Ps. xci. 11; Heb. i. 14.
3. When Jacob saw them, what did he say? Gen. xxxii. 2.
4. What is the meaning of Mahanaim? *Ans.* Two hosts or camps.
5. Whom did Jacob send to Esau, his brother? Gen. xxxii. 3.
6. What message did he send by them? Gen. xxxii. 4, 5.
7. What tidings did the messengers bring back? Gen. xxxii. 6.
8. How was Jacob affected? Gen. xxxii. 7, f. c.
9. Why was he greatly distressed?
10. What measures did he adopt for his safety? Gen. xxxii. 7, 8.
11. What prayer did he offer up? Gen. xxxii. 9–11.
12. What promise did he present before God? Gen. xxxi. 3, 13.
13. What other promise did he refer to? Gen. xxxii. 12.
14. When was this made? Gen. xxviii. 13, 14, 15.
15. What present did Jacob prepare for his brother? Gen. xxxii. 13–16.
16. What directions did Jacob give to his servants? Gen. xxxii. 17–19.
17. Why did he send before him the presents? Gen. xxxii. 20

18. What did he do with his family? Gen. xxxii. 22, 23.

19. What took place when Jacob was left alone? Gen. xxxii. 24, 25.

20. Was this a physical or spiritual struggle? Hosea xii. 4, 5.

21. What did Jacob say to the angel? Gen. xxxii. 26.

22. What duty does this teach us? Hosea xii. 6.

23. To what was Jacob's name changed? Gen. xxxii. 28.

24. Why was it changed? Gen. xxxii. 28.

25. What did Jacob call the place? Gen. xxxii. 30.

26. What is the meaning of Peniel? *Ans.* Face of God.

27. What comfort did Jacob receive? Gen. xxxii. 30, l. c.

28. How is the memory of what happened to Jacob's thigh preserved among the Jews? Gen. xxxii. 32.

29. How did Jacob approach his brother? Gen. xxxiii. 1–3.

30. How did Esau receive him? Gen. xxxiii. 4.

31. How did Jacob show his anxiety to be fully reconciled to his brother? Gen. xxxiii. 8–11.

32. How did Jacob show his care for his children and flocks? Gen. xxxiii. 13, 14.

33. Whither did Jacob go? Gen. xxxiii. 17.

34. To what place did he next remove? Gen xxxiii. 18.

35. What religious act did he perform? Gen xxxiii. 20.

36. What is the meaning of El-elohe-Israel? *Ans* God, the God of Israel.

LESSON XII.

JOSEPH, THE BELOVED BOY SOLD INTO SLAVERY.

1. Where did Jacob dwell? Gen. xxxvii. 1.
2. How old was Joseph at the time this narrative commences? Gen. xxxvii. 2.
3. What report did he bring to his father? Gen. xxxvii. 2, l. c.
4. How did Israel show his affection for him? Gen. xxxvii. 3.
5. How many sons had Jacob, and what were their names? Gen. xxxv. 22–26.
6. How did Joseph's brethren feel toward him? Gen. xxxvii. 4.
7. What increased their hatred? Gen. xxxvii. 5–8.
8. What was his next dream? Gen. xxxvii. 9.
9. How did his father apply this? Gen. xxxvii. 10
10. Whence came these dreams?
11. Whither did Joseph's brethren go to feed the flock? Gen. xxxvii. 12.
12. What directions did Israel give to Joseph? Gen. xxxvii. 13, 14.
13. How far was Shechem from Hebron? *Ans.* About sixty miles.
14. Where did Joseph find his brethren? Gen. xxxvii. 15-17.
15. How far distant was Dothan from Shechem? *Ans.* The distance is not known with absolute certainty. Probably about ten miles.
16. What did Joseph's brethren do when they saw him afar off? Gen. xxxvii. 18.
17. Can you cite other instances of the conspiracies

of wicked men? 1 Sam. xix. 1; Ps. xxxi. 13; Matt. xxvii. 1; Acts xxiii. 12.

18. What did Reuben propose, to save the life of his brother? Gen. xxxvii. 21, 22.

19. What was done with Joseph? Gen. xxxvii. 23, 24.

20. How was he affected by their cruel treatment? Gen xlii. 21.

21. What next became a link in the chain of divine providences? Gen. xxxvii. 25.

22. What plan did Judah propose? Gen. xxxvii. 26, 27.

23. What bargain was made for Joseph? Gen. xxxvii. 28.

24. Was this the first person ever sold into slavery? *Ans.* This is the first recorded instance of the sale of a human being, although it is probable that the sin had long been practised.

25. What prompted his brothers to sell him? Acts vii. 9.

26. How was Reuben affected when he discovered that Joseph was missing? Gen. xxxvii. 29, 30.

27. What did the cruel men do to hide their guilt? Gen. xxxvii. 31, 32.

28. What great falsehood did they tell? Gen. xxxvii. 32, l. c.

29. What four sins did they commit, one after another? Gen. xxxvii. 4, 18, 28, 32.

30. How did the treatment that Christ received resemble that of Joseph? John xv. 24; Matt. xxvii. 9.

31. How was Jacob affected when he saw the coat? Gen. xxxvii. 33, 34.

32. What is sackcloth? *Ans.* A coarse sack, made sometimes of camels' hair.

33. What was done to comfort Jacob? Gen. xxxvii. 35.

34. What additional sin did the sons here commit?

35. To whom was Joseph sold by the Midianites? Gen. xxxvii. 36.

36. What was the captain of the guard? *Ans.* The chief marshal, or chief of the king's slaughter men, or executioners.

LESSON XIII.

JOSEPH.—A LIGHT IN A PRISON.

1. To what country was Joseph brought? Gen. xxxix. 1.

2. At what period was this? *Ans.* About 1729 B. C.

3. What is the meaning of the name Pharaoh? *Ans.* It was the common name given to the Egyptian kings, and signified sovereign power.

4. For what was Egypt early distinguished?

5. What can you say of its agricultural resources? Gen. xii. 10; xlii. 2; xli. 47, 48.

6. What caused Joseph to prosper, though he was a slave? Gen. xxxix. 2.

7. To what office was he elevated? Gen. xxxix. 4.

8. What effect had the presence of Joseph upon the Egyptian court and country? Gen. xxxix. 5.

9. What must Joseph's life have been, to have produced these results?

10. What was Joseph's personal appearance? Gen. xxxix. 6.

11. What did he say when tempted to sin? Gen. xxxix. 9.

12. Against whom is sin always committed? 2 Sam. xii. 13; Ps. li. 4.

13. Who is wronged by every sin? Prov. viii. 36.

14. What false accusation was brought against Joseph? Gen. xxxix. 17, 18.

15. What unjust punishment was inflicted upon Joseph? Gen. xxxix. 20.

16. Did the Lord forsake the slave and the prisoner? Gen. xxxix. 21.

17. Did Joseph cease to be useful because this calamity had come upon him? Gen. xxxix. 22, 23.

18. Why was he specially praiseworthy? 1 Peter ii. 19.

19. What conduct is acceptable to God? 1 Peter ii. 20.

20. What was the next link in the chain of divine providence? Gen. xl. 1–5.

21. What office did the butler fill? Neh. i. 11, l. c.

22. Why were the offices of butler and baker to the king very responsible offices?

23. To whom do the interpretations of dreams belong? Gen. xl. 8; Dan. ii. 20–22.

24. How are God's servants enabled to interpret dreams?

25. What was the dream of the chief butler? Gen. xl. 9–11.

26. What was the interpretation of it? Gen. xl. 12, 13.

27. What request did Joseph make? Gen. xl. 14.

28. Did Joseph declare his innocence? Gen. xl. 15

29. What was the dream of the chief baker? Gen. xl. 16, 17.

30. How was this interpreted? Gen. xl. 18, 19.

31. Did the declarations of Joseph become true Gen. xl. 20–22.

32. What did this prove? 1 Chron. xxviii. 9; Ps xxv. 14.

33. Did the chief butler, on being restored to office, remember Joseph? Gen. xl. 23

34. Are persons in affliction often forgotten? Job xix. 14; Ps. xxxi. 12.

35. Who remembers those who confide in him? Luke xxiii. 42, 43.

36. What lessons does this narrative teach us?

LESSON XIV.

JOSEPH, GOD'S SERVANT IN A HEATHEN PALACE.

1. How long was Joseph kept in prison after the chief butler was restored to office? Gen. xli. 1.

2. In what year was this? *Ans.* 1715 B. C.

3. What remarkable dream had Pharaoh? Gen. xli. 1–4.

4. Whence came this dream?

5. Can you give other instances of divine communications being made through dreams?

6. What river is here referred to? *Ans.* The Nile.

7. Give some account of the Nile.

8. What other dream had Pharaoh? Gen. xli. 5–7.

9. Whom did the king send for, to interpret his dreams? Gen. xli. 8.

10. Give some account of these magicians and wise men.

11. Why could they not explain the dreams?

12. How was Joseph brought to the notice of Pharaoh? Gen. xli. 9–13.

13. Describe the first interview between Joseph and the king. Gen. xli. 14, 15.

14. To whom does Joseph ascribe the power to interpret dreams? Gen. xli. 16.

15. Mention some other instances of dependence

upon God. Dan. ii. 20–22; Acts iii. 12, 13; 2 Cor. iii. 5.

16. What did Joseph say when he heard the dreams? Gen. xli. 25.

17. What did he mean by their being one?

18. What explanations did Joseph give of the dreams? Gen. xli. 26–31.

19. What is there peculiar about the use of the number seven in the Scriptures?

20. Why was the dream "doubled unto Pharaoh"? Gen. xli. 32.

21. Does God always bring to pass his purposes?

22. Does he often make use, in this, of the acts of free agents?

23. Could you mention any instances of this, in the history of Joseph?

24. What excellent advice did Joseph give to Pharaoh? Gen. xli. 33–36.

25. How did Pharaoh receive it? Gen. xli. 37.

26. What led the king to place such full confidence in the words of Joseph? Gen. xli. 13, 39.

27. Whom did the king appoint to the important office? Gen. xli. 40, 41.

28. What great honors were conferred upon Joseph? Gen. xli. 42, 43.

29. What name did Pharaoh give to Joseph? Gen. xli. 45.

30. What does this mean? *Ans.* The revealer of secrets.

31. How old was Joseph at this time? Gen. xli. 46

32. How old was he when sold by his brethren? Gen. xxxvii. 2.

33. How long was he in slavery?

34. How did Joseph show his perfect confidence in the truth of his interpretation of the dreams? Gen. xli. 48, 49.

35. What names did Joseph give to his children? Gen. xli. 51, 52

36. What followed the seven years of plenty? Gen. xli. 54, 55.

37. What regulated the crops in Egypt? *Ans.* The rise of the waters of the Nile. When they rose only twelve cubits, the crops failed and famine ensued. When they rose from fourteen to sixteen cubits, the whole country was watered through canals, and the crops were abundant.

38. What important practical lessons does this part of Joseph's history teach us?

LESSON XV.

JOSEPH, THE SLAVE, EXALTED TO BE A PRINCE.

1. What was another link in the chain of divine providences? Gen. xlii. 1, 2.

2. Had Canaan been afflicted with famine before this time? Gen. xii. 10; xxvi. 1.

3. How many of Joseph's brethren went down to Egypt? Gen. xlii. 3, 4.

4. How did they approach Joseph? Gen. xlii. 6.

5. What prophetic dream was thus fulfilled? Gen. xxxvii. 7.

6. How were these men who endeavored to defeat the dream, the agents for its fulfilment?

7. How did Joseph treat them? Gen. xlii. 7–9.

8. Why did he treat them roughly?

9. What did he mean by saying, "Ye are spies"?

10. What account did they give of themselves? Gen. xlii 10, 11, 13.

11. What did they mean by saying, "One is not"?

12. How did Joseph propose to test the truth of what they had said? Gen. xlii. 15, 16.

13. What punishment did he inflict upon them? Gen. xlii. 17.

14. What effect did this treatment have? Gen. xlii. 21.

15. Were these calamities just what they deserved and needed?

16. What did Reuben say? Gen. xlii. 22.

17. Did they recognize Joseph? Gen. xlii. 23.

18. How long was it since they sold him? *Ans.* About 22 years.

19. Why did Joseph speak to his brethren by an interpreter?

20. How was Joseph affected by their conversation? Gen. xlii. 24.

21. What occurred on the journey home? Gen. xlii. 25–28.

22. Describe the home scene on their arrival. Gen. xlii. 35–38.

23. Did Jacob afterward allow Benjamin to go with his brethren? Gen. xliii. 11–13.

24. How did Joseph receive them this time? Gen. xliii. 26–34.

25. What was the steward commanded to do? Gen. xliv. 1–5.

26. What startling discovery was made on the homeward journey? Gen. xliv. 6–12.

27. Give an account of the return. Gen. xliv. 13–17.

28. What eloquent and touching appeal did Judah make for his young brother? Gen. xliv. 18–34.

29. How was Joseph affected? Gen. xlv. 1, 2.

30. How did he make himself known to his brethren? Gen. xlv. 3, 4.

31. Why were they troubled at his presence?

32. What did Joseph say to comfort them? Gen. xlv. 5–13.

33. How did he show his affection for Benjamin? Gen. xlv. 14.

34. How did he manifest the spirit of forgiveness toward all his brethren? Gen. xlv. 15.

35. What lessons does this part of the history of Joseph teach us?

LESSON XVI.

JOSEPH, THE AFFECTIONATE SON.

1. What proof is there that Joseph was highly esteemed in the court of Pharaoh? Gen. xlv. 16.

2. What directions did the king give? Gen. xlv. 17, 18.

3. How did Joseph show his brotherly affection? Gen. xlv. 21, 22.

4. Why did he give so much to Benjamin?

5. What did he send to his father? Gen. xlv. 23.

6. What good advice did he give to the brothers? Gen. xlv. 24.

7. Why did he thus caution them?

8. Describe the arrival home. Gen. xlv. 25–28.

9. What precious promises were made to Israel? Gen. xlvi. 2–4.

10. What great promises had been made to the other patriarchs?

11. Describe the journey to Egypt. Gen. xlvi. 5–7.

12. How did the noble son receive his father? Gen. xlvi. 28, 29.

13. Describe the interview with Pharaoh. Gen. xlvii. 1–10.

14. What provision did Joseph make for the family? Gen. xlvii. 11, 12.

15. What request was made of Joseph? Gen. xlvii. 29, 30.

16. Did he promise to comply? Gen. xlvii. 30, 31.

17. What blessing did Jacob bestow upon Joseph and his sons? Gen. xlviii. 15, 16, 20, 21.

18. How was Joseph affected by the death of his father? Gen. l. 1, 2.

19. What proof is there that the father greatly loved this son? Gen. xxxvii. 3, 33, 34; xlv. 28; xlvi. 30.

20. How long did the Egyptians mourn for Jacob? Gen. l. 3.

21. What distinguished honors were paid to Jacob? Gen. l. 7–9.

22. Why was he followed to the grave by such an imposing procession?

23. Where was there a great mourning for him? Gen. l. 10, 11.

24. What is the meaning of Abel-mizraim? *Ans.* The mourning of the Egyptians.

25. Where was Jacob buried? Gen. l. 13.

26. Whither did Joseph go after the burial? Gen. l. 14.

27. What did Joseph's brethren now fear? Gen. l 15.

28. Had they any just reasons for such fears?

29. What did they do to obtain forgiveness? Gen l. 16, 17.

30. How was the noble brother affected by the appeal? Gen. l. 17, l. c.

31. What prophecy was fulfilled in Gen. l. 18?

32. How do the great excellencies of Joseph's character shine forth? Gen. l. 19–21.

33. How long did Joseph live? Gen. l. 22.

34. What divine promise did he express to his brethren? Gen. l. 24.

35. Where did he desire to be buried?

36. Why is it mentioned, Gen. l. 26, that he was put in a coffin? *Ans.* Because this was a distinguished honor in Egypt.

37. Let the class state the several important practical lessons that the history of Joseph teaches.

LESSON XVII.

MOSES.—THE PLEASURES OF A PALACE RELINQUISHED FOR THE SERVICE OF GOD.

1. Who were the children of Israel? Ex. i. 1–4.
2. Trace the genealogy of Moses. Ex. vi. 16–20.
3. After the death of Joseph and his brethren, how numerous did the Israelites become? Ex. i. 7.
4. What means were adopted to keep down their power? Ex. i. 8–11.
5. Were these means successful? Ex. i. 12.
6. What peculiar hardships did they suffer? Ex. i. 13, 14.
7. What cruel order did Pharaoh issue? Ex. i. 22.
8. How did the infant Moses escape the power of this wicked decree? Ex. ii. 1–4.
9. How was the providence of God shown in his preservation? Ex. ii. 5–9.
10. Why was he called Moses? Ex. ii. 10.
11. What did Moses learn at the court of Pharaoh? Acts vii. 22.
12. What providential design do we discover in these facts?
13. What resolution did Moses form when "he was come to years"? Heb. xi. 24.

14. What noble choice did he make? Heb. xi. 25.
15. Was this a wise choice?
16. What other saints have made it?
17. What did Moses esteem greater riches than the treasures of Egypt? Heb. xi. 26.
18. How did he reap the results of this principle?
19. When did he show his sympathy for his oppressed brethren? Ex. ii. 11, 12.
20. Is it probable that he often witnessed the great cruelty of the task-masters?
21. Under whose authority did he feel that he was acting, in thus taking the part of the oppressed? Acts vii. 24, 25.
22. What did the king do when he heard of this deed? Ex. ii. 15, f. c.
23. What course did Moses take? Ex. ii. 15, l. c.
24. How old was he at this time? Acts vii. 23.
25. How is the providence of God farther illustrated in his history? Ex. ii. 16–21.
26. What was the condition of the Hebrews at this time? Ex. ii. 23.
27. How did God show his compassion? Ex. ii. 24, 25.
28. How long was Moses a shepherd in Midian? Acts vii. 30.
29. How did God prepare him, during this period, for his service?
30. How many years was Moses receiving his education for his important mission as the deliverer of God's people? Acts vii. 23, 30.
31. Why was it necessary that so much time should be taken for his discipline and education?
32. What lesson is here taught us?

LESSON XVIII

MOSES, THE DELIVERER OF GOD'S PEOPLE.

1. To what mount did Moses lead his flock? Ex iii. 1.
2. Why was this called the Mount of God? Ex iii. 12; I Kings xix. 8.
3. Who appeared unto Moses? Ex. iii. 2.
4. Was this an ordinary angel? Ex. iii. 4; Acts vii. 30, 31.
5. What announcement was made to Moses? Ex. iii. 6.
6. Did God appear in any form to Moses? Deut. iv. 15.
7. Why did he never appear in any shape, or similitude of any object? Deut. iv. 15–19.
8. What promise did God make to Moses? Ex. iii. 7, 8.
9. To what service was Moses appointed? Ex. iii. 10.
10. What did Moses say in reply? Ex. iii. 11.
11. How did the Lord encourage him? Ex. iii. 12.
12. By what token was he to make known his authority? Ex. iii. 12-14; vi. 3.
13. To whom is the "I am" also applied? John viii. 58.
14. What aid was promised to Moses in his work? Ex. iii. 19, 20.
15. How were the people directed to make some provision for their journey? Ex. iii. 21, 22.
16. Will you give more precisely the meaning of the language of the 22d verse? *Ans.* But every woman shall require, or demand of her neighbor, etc.,

jewels of silver, etc., and ye shall put them upon your sons and your daughters: and thus ye shall obtain from the Egyptians some remuneration for your long and arduous services.

17. Was it right to make this demand? *Ans.* It certainly was; for these hundreds of thousands of Israelites had probably not been allowed to accumulate any property, but had been compelled to give all their gains to their oppressors.

18. By what signs was Moses to show the divine authority under which he acted? Ex. iv. 1–9.

19. How was Moses received by the elders and the people? Ex. iv. 29–31.

20. How did Pharaoh receive his proposition? Ex. v. 1, 2.

21. What additional burdens were put upon the oppressed Israelites? Ex. v. 6–9.

22. How did Moses present the case to the Lord? Ex. v. 22, 23.

23. In what language did the Lord address Moses? Ex. vi. 2–5.

24. What was he directed to say from the Lord to the children of Israel? Ex. vi. 6–8.

25. What commission did God give to Moses in regard to Pharaoh? Gen. vii. 1, 2.

26. In what sense was Moses a "god to Pharaoh"? Ex. iv. 16, l. c.; Jer. i. 10.

27. What did God say that he would do to Pharaoh? Ex. vii. 3.

28. What does this language mean? *Ans.* God would permit Pharaoh's heart to be hardened.

29. Who was the real agent in producing this hardness of heart? Ex. ix. 34; x. 16, 17.

30. Does God ever tempt men to sin? James i. 13.

31. After a series of mighty miracles had been wrought which displayed the power of God, what did the Lord say to Moses? Ex. xiv. 1–4.

32. When it was told the king that the people had fled, what did he do? Ex. xiv. 5–9.

33. Does not every man who oppresses his fellow men rush against the omnipotent justice of God?

34. How were the fugitives preserved? Ex. xiv. 19–22.

35. Did the proud and maddened oppressors follow after them? Ex. xiv. 23.

36. Whence did trouble come to them? Ex. xiv. 24.

37. What discovery did the oppressors make? Ex. xiv. 25, l. c.

38. What was their fate? Ex. xiv. 26–28.

39. What principles triumphed here?

40. How did mercy triumph? Ex. xiv. 29, 30.

41. How were the Israelites impressed by these scenes? Ex. xiv. 31.

42. What lessons do you learn from them?

LESSON XIX.

MOSES, THE LEADER IN THE WILDERNESS.

1. How long did the children of Israel dwell in the land of Egypt? Ex. xii. 40.

2. How was their deliverance celebrated? Ex. xv. 1, 2.

3. Whither did Moses lead them after the over throw of the Egyptians? Ex. xv. 22.

4. What course did Moses take when the people complained to him? Ex. xv. 24, 25.

5. Have we the same encouragement to go to God for counsel and aid that Moses had? Matt. vii. 7, 8; xxi. 22; John xiv. 13; xv. 7.

6. What trial had Moses in the wilderness? Ex xvi. 2, 3

7. What virtue did he specially need? James i. 4.

8. How did the Lord promise to supply the people with food? Ex. xvi. 4, 5.

9. Was the promise fulfilled? Ex. xvi. 13–15.

10. How did Moses enforce the observance of the Sabbath? Ex. xvi. 22–26.

11. How did God distinctly teach the duty of observing the Sabbath? Ex. xvi. 27–29.

12. What was the next trial that befell Moses? Ex. xvii. 2, 3.

13. To whom did he go for counsel? Ex. xvii. 4.

14. What miracle was he directed to perform? Ex. xvii. 5, 6.

15. How did God assist Moses in conquering the foes of the Israelites? Ex. xvii. 8–13.

16. How was this event commemorated? Ex. xvii. 14–16.

17. Was the prediction in regard to Amalek fulfilled? 1 Sam. xv. 3, etc.

18. What is the meaning of Jehovah-nissi? *Ans.* Jehovah is my ensign, or banner.

19. What important announcement was made to Moses? Ex. xix. 10–13.

20. Describe the solemn scene upon Mount Sinai. Ex. xix. 16–20.

21. What laws were communicated from God, through Moses, to mankind? Ex. xx. 1–17.

22. Are these all binding now?

23. What proofs are there that the Sabbath was observed before these commandments were given? Ex. xvi. 25; xx. 8; xxxi. 13; Lev. xix. 3.

24. What was the appearance of Moses when he again came down from the mount? Ex. xxxiv. 29–32; 2 Cor. iii. 7.

25. When did he again appear radiant with glory? Matt. xvii. 3, 4.

26. For what virtues was Moses distinguished? Num. xii. 3; Heb. xi. 27.

27. On what occasion did he speak unadviseoly? Num. xx. 10; Ps. cvi. 32, 33.
28. How was Moses reproved for his sin? Num. xx. 12.
29. Why was Moses not permitted to enter the promised land? Deut. xxxii. 51, 52.
30. Give an account of the death of this noble servant of God. Deut. xxxiv. 1–5.
31. What is said of him at the time of his death? Deut. xxxiv. 7.
32. How is his great name honored? John i. 17; v. 46; Acts vii. 35.
33. For what is the world indebted to Moses?
34. In what should we imitate him?

LESSON XX

AARON, THE PRIEST OF GOD.

1. To what service was the tribe of Levi appointed? Num. iii. 5–8.
2. What was Aaron called? Ex. iv. 14.
3. What service was he to render to Moses? Ex. iv. 16.
4. What success did he meet with in speaking to the people? Ex. iv. 30, 31.
5. What gave him success? Ex. vii. 6
6. How old was Aaron at this time? Ex. vii. 7.
7. Who were appointed priests with him? Ex. xxviii. 1.
8. What garments did the Lord direct Moses to have prepared for the priests? Ex. xxviii. 2–4.
9. Describe the breastplate of judgment. Ex. xxviii. 15–21.

10. What names was Aaron to bear upon the breastplate of judgment? Ex. xxviii. 29.

11. What was to be engraved upon a plate of pure gold? Ex. xxviii. 36.

12. What did God require of those who filled the office of priest? Ex. xix. 22; Ps. cxxxii. 9; Is. lii. 11.

13. What were some of their duties? Ex. xxx. 7-10; Heb. v. 1.

14. Were others besides the Levites allowed to perform the duties of priests? Num. iii. 9, 10.

15. How was Aaron tempted when Moses was in the mount? Ex. xxxii. 1.

16. Did he yield to the temptation? Ex. xxxii. 2-4.

17. Is it probable that he intended to overthrow the worship of the Lord? Ex. xxxii. 5.

18. What was the result of his course? Ex. xxxii. 6-8.

19. With what feelings did God regard this sin of Aaron? Deut. ix. 20.

20. What excuse did Aaron give for his conduct? Ex. xxxii. 22.

21. Was this a good excuse?

22. What ought he to have done when the wicked proposition was made to him?

23. Was Aaron permitted to enter the promised land? Num. xx. 24.

24. Where did he die? Num. xx. 27, 28.

25. How old was he at the time of his death? Num xxxiii. 39.

26. Who is now our great High-priest? Heb vi. 20.

27. How long is his priesthood to continue? Heb vii. 24.

28. Why is there no need of any other priest?

29. How great is his power to save men? Heb vii 25.

30. What is his character? Heb. vii. 26

31. What is our duty, since we have such an High-priest? Heb. x. 19–23.

32. To what sacred profession are Christians admitted? 1 Peter ii. 5, 9.

33. To whom belongs all the glory for these great honors? Rev. i. 5, 6.

LESSON XXI.

JOSHUA, THE RESOLUTE HERO.

1. Whom did God appoint to lead the children of Israel across the river Jordan? Josh. i. 1, 2.
2. How many days after the death of Moses was the appointment made? Deut. xxxiv. 8.
3. What is the meaning of Joshua?
4. By what name is he called in Acts vii. 45?
5. Of whom was Joshua a type?
6. What was his name at first? Num. xiii. 8, 16.
7. What distinguished privileges had he enjoyed in connection with Moses? Ex. xxxii. 15–18.
8. How was he qualified for the great work before him?
9. What miracles had he witnessed in connection with the journeys of the Israelites?
10. What important services had he rendered? Ex. xvii. 9–13.
11. How much land was promised to Joshua? Josh. i. 3, 4.
12. What is the "great sea" here referred to?
13. How old was Joshua at this time? *Ans.* Eighty-four years.

14. What charge did God give to him? Josh i. 6

15. What was the secret of his strength? Josh i. 5, l. c.

16. What ought we to be able boldly to say? Heb xiii. 6.

17. Upon what does every man's prosperity depend? Josh. i. 7.

18. Is it sufficient to read the law? Josh. i. 8.

19. What orders did Joshua issue to the people Josh. i. 10, 11.

20. How did he know that they would pass over Jordan within three days?

21. Did the people confide in their new leader? Josh. i. 16, 17.

22. What preparations were made for the great event before them? Josh. iii. 1-6.

23. What did the Lord say to Joshua? Josh. iii. 7.

24. What was the symbol of the divine presence and power? Josh. iii. 11.

25. Describe the passage across the Jordan. Josh. iii. 14-17.

26. What did Joshua direct to be done as a memorial of this event? Josh. iv. 4-7.

27. How did the people regard their leader after this great miracle? Josh. iv. 14.

28. What occurred after the priests came up out of the river? Josh. iv. 18.

29. What was the design of this miracle? Josh iv. 24.

30. What is the design of all the miracles recorded in the Old Testament?

31. What elements of character did Joshua display on this occasion?

LESSON XXII.

JOSHUA, THE CONQUEROR IN GOD'S NAME.

1. What impression did the passage over the Jordan make upon the kings of the heathen? Josh. v. 1.
2. How did Joshua show his coolness and bravery? Josh. v. 13.
3. Who was the being that appeared before him? Josh. v. 14; Ex. xxiii. 23.
4. What did the "captain of the Lord's host" say? Josh. v. 15. Comp. Ex. iii. 5; Acts vii. 33.
5. What city did the Lord promise to deliver to Joshua? Josh. vi. 2.
6. How was Jericho taken? Josh. vi. 12–16, 20.
7. How extensive was the punishment inflicted? Josh. vi. 21.
8. Why was the destruction so complete? Deut. vii. 2–4.
9. What was done with the silver and gold? Josh. vi. 19.
10. What rigid commands were given by God? Josh. vi. 18; Deut. vii. 24, 26; xiii. 17.
11. Why were these orders so strict?
12. Did any of the Israelites disobey? Josh. vii. 1.
13. What disaster followed this act of disobedience? Josh. vii. 2–5.
14. Why did others suffer for Achan's sin?
15. How was Joshua affected? Josh. vii. 6–9.
16. What punishment was threatened against the evil-doer? Josh. vii. 13–15.
17. Did Achan confess his sin? Josh. vii. 19–21.
18. What did Joshua then do? Josh. vii. 22–24.
19 How was Achan punished? Josh. vii. 25.

20. What was the object of these wars and these severe measures against transgressors? *Ans.* To utterly destroy idolatry, and keep the children of Israel from "the accursed thing."

21. Did Joshua obtain other victories? Josh. viii. 1, 25, 28.

22. How did he celebrate his victories? Josh. viii. 30, 31.

23. What motives guided Joshua in the prosecution of their wars?

24. How were the Israelites guarded against the spirit of avarice or revenge?

25. How must we regard these wars? *Ans.* As God's judgments against the abominations of heathenism.

26. How many kings did Joshua subdue? Josh. xii.

27. What did Joshua say to the elders and others, in his old age? Josh. xxiii. 4, 5.

28. What advice did he give to them? Josh. xxiii 6–8.

29. What noble testimony did our hero bear to God's faithfulness? Josh. xxiii. 14.

30. What did he say to the people? Josh. xxiv. 14.

31. What would be the consequence, should they forsake God? Josh. xxiv. 20.

32. Are these principles applicable to nations now?

33. Give an account of the death of Joshua. Josh. xxiv. 29, 30.

34. What can you say of his influence? Josh. xxiv. 31

LESSON XXIII.

SAMUEL. — EARLY CONSECRATION TO GOD.

1. Who was the mother of Samuel? 1 Sam. i. 20.
2. What was the character of Hannah?
3. To whom did she purpose to dedicate her child? 1 Sam. i. 22.
4. What was done with Samuel when he was very young? 1 Sam. i. 24, 25.
5. Who was Eli?
6. What did Hannah say to Eli? 1 Sam. i. 26–28.
7. What did she mean by saying, "I have lent him to the Lord"?
8. What is the duty of parents to their children? Deut. vi. 7; xi. 18, 19.
9. Why should this duty be performed? Ps. lxxviii. 7.
10. What is God's desire? Deut. v. 29.
11. How did the mother of Samuel express her joy and gratitude to God? 1 Sam. ii. 1.
12. Over whose birth should we greatly rejoice? Is. ix. 6.
13. What did Samuel do, "being a child"? 1 Sam. ii. 18.
14. What services did he probably perform?
15. Who, under God, guided the destiny of this child? 1 Sam. ii. 20.
16. What is the duty of parents, in regard to consecrating their children to the service of God, in the gospel ministry?
17. Will such parents be blessed? 1 Sam. ii. 20.
18. Did the mother of Samuel forget her little boy, though he was from home? 1 Sam. ii. 19.
19. Whose favor did Samuel obtain? 1 Sam. ii. 26.

20. How did he gain this favor?
21. Who was probably daily praying for him at home?
22. Give an account of God's first communication to Samuel. 1 Sam. iii. 1–10.
23. What did the Lord say to Samuel? 1 Sam. iii. 11–14.
24. How was Samuel affected? 1 Sam. iii. 15.
25. What did Eli ask him? 1 Sam. iii. 16, 17.
26. What reply did Samuel make? 1 Sam. iii. 18, f. c.
27. How did the aged priest receive it? 1 Sam. iii. 18, l. c.
28. What two offices did Samuel hold? 1 Sam. iii. 20; vii. 15.
29. For what was he eminent as a judge? 1 Sam. xii. 3.
30. How did the people regard him? 1 Sam. xii. 4, 5.
31. Had Samuel power with God? 1 Sam. vii. 9, 10.
32. What did Samuel, as prophet and judge, accomplish for the children of Israel?

LESSON XXIV

SAUL, THE FIRST KING OF ISRAEL.

1. What was the character of Samuel's sons? 1 Sam. viii. 1–3.
2. Why did the elders of Israel desire a king? 1 Sam. viii. 4, 5.
3. How did Samuel receive the proposition? 1 Sam viii. 6.

4. Why did the thing displease him? *Ans.* Because it was a renunciation of the government of Heaven.

5. What did the Lord say to Samuel? 1 Sam. viii. 7.

6. With what feelings did God grant their request?

7. Under what protest was a king to be given? 1 Sam. viii. 9.

8. What were they to receive with the king? 1 Sam. viii. 11-18.

9. Who is the best king that we can have to rule over us?

10. What advantages will come to us from selecting God as our king? Ps. xviii. 2; xxvii. 1; xlvi. 1-4.

11. Who was appointed to be the first king over Israel? 1 Sam. ix. 17.

12. How did Samuel anoint Saul? 1 Sam. x. 1.

13. What promises were made to the new king? 1 Sam. x. 6, 7.

14. How was Saul received by the people? 1 Sam. x. 24.

15. What did Samuel tell the people? 1 Sam. x. 25.

16. What did he write in a book? Deut. xvii. 14-20.

17. Upon what conditions were the people to receive prosperity? 1 Sam. xii. 13-15.

18. Did the king obey the commands of God? 1 Sam. xiii. 11-13.

19. What would be the consequence of his sin? 1 Sam. xiii. 14.

20. On what occasion did Saul again disobey? 1 Sam. xv. 3, 9.

21. What excuse did he give for his conduct? 1 Sam. xv. 20, 21.

22. What does God desire more than sacrifices? 1 Sam. xv. 22.

23. Whom did Saul fear? 1 Sam. xv. 24.

24. Whom ought we to fear?

25. What were the personal consequences to him of departing from God? 1 Sam. xvi. 14.

26. What became of his kingdom? 1 Sam. xv. 28.

27. Who was to succeed Saul upon the throne? 1 Sam. xvi. 1.

28. How was Saul comforted? 1 Sam. xvi. 23.

29. How did he at first regard David? 1 Sam. xvi. 21.

30. What did he attempt to do to him after his jealousy was excited? 1 Sam. xviii. 10, 11; xix. 1.

31. What other sins did he commit? 1 Sam. xxii. 17–19.

32. How did the wicked king show his folly after God had deserted him? 1 Sam. xxviii. 7, 8.

33. Did he sin in this? Deut. xviii. 9–12.

34. What is the effect of sin upon the intellect as well as the heart?

35. How was Saul punished? 1 Chron. x. 13, 14.

36. What was the manner of his death? 1 Sam xxxi. 3, 4.

37. How was his body dishonored? 1 Sam. xxxi 8–10.

38. What lessons are we taught by the career and end of Saul?

LESSON XXV.

JONATHAN, THE HEROIC FRIEND.

1. Who was Jonathan? 1 Sam. xix. 1, 2.
2. What were his claims to the throne of Israel?
3. What reason had he to be jealous of David? 1 Sam. xvi. 1, l. c.
4. What were his feelings toward David? 1 Sam. xviii. 1.
5. How did he display his noble and exalted friendship? 1 Sam. xviii. 4.
6. Was it customary in the East for one to show his love for another in this way?
7. What attractive qualities had David? 1 Sam xviii. 14.
8. Were the wicked attracted by the piety and wisdom of David? 1 Sam. xviii. 12, 15.
9. How was David generally regarded? 1 Sam. xviii. 16.
10. What important service did Jonathan render to David? 1 Sam. xix. 1–3.
11. How did he plead for him? 1 Sam. xix. 4, 5.
12. What are the tests of true friendship?
13. What is the meaning of Jonathan?
14. What effect did Jonathan's appeal have upon his father? 1 Sam. xix. 6.
15. Did Saul keep his promise? 1 Sam. xix. 8–10.
16. How did Jonathan show still further his affection for David? 1 Sam. xx. 4, 12–15.
17. What did they make together? 1 Sam. xx. 16.
18. What is a covenant?
19. How strong was the love of Jonathan for David? 1 Sam. xx. 17.
20 What love surpasses this. John iii. 16

21. How did the two friends show their affection? 1 Sam. xx. 41.

22. What parting words were uttered? 1 Sam. xx. 42.

23. Did they meet again? 1 Sam. xxxi. 2.

24. With what feelings did David receive the tidings of the death of his friend? 2 Sam. i. 11, 12.

25. In what language was the lamentation over the fallen expressed? 2 Sam. i. 19–22.

26. In what beautiful language was the friendship between the two expressed? 2 Sam. i. 23, 26.

27. Will you give another instance of true friendship? Ruth i. 16, 17.

28. How does the conduct of Saul appear in contrast with that of his noble son?

29. What were the characteristics of Jonathan's friendship?

30. What must we do to secure friends? Prov. xviii. 24.

31. Whose friendship should we aim to secure?

LESSON XXVI.

DAVID, THE YOUTHFUL CHAMPION OF THE HOSTS OF ISRAEL.

1. What is the meaning of the name David?
2. In what year of the world was David born?
3. Where was he born?
4. Who was his father?
5. What was his employment in early life? 1 Sam. xvi. 11.
6. What other distinguished Bible heroes had been shepherds?

7. By whom was David appointed to be king over Israel? 1 Sam. xvi. 1.

8. Through whom had God ruled Israel before he gave kings to the nation?

9. What did the Lord say to Samuel, his prophet? 1 Sam. xvi. 7.

10. What practical lesson does this verse teach us?

11. Describe the scene when the youthful David was anointed. 1 Sam. xvi. 8–13.

12. Was the fact of the consecration of David to be king generally known at this time?

13. What occurred when David was about twenty years of age? 1 Sam. xvii. 1–3.

14. What champion went out from the camp of the Philistines? 1 Sam. xvii. 4–7.

15. What challenge did he utter? 1 Sam. xvii. 8–10.

16. How were the Israelites affected by it? 1 Sam xvii. 11.

17. When did David first see Goliath? 1 Sam xvii. 20–23.

18. What did David say to King Saul? 1 Sam. xvii. 32.

19. What did Saul say to David? 1 Sam. xvii. 33.

20. What proof did David give of his valor? 1 Sam. xvii. 34–36.

21. What proof did he give of his confidence in God? 1 Sam. xvii. 37.

22. What principle inspired him at this time?

23. What preparation did he at first make for the conflict? 1 Sam. xvii. 38, 39.

24. What did he take with him? 1 Sam. xvii. 40.

25. What constituted his defences? Ps. xviii. 2.

26. With what armor was he clothed? Eph. vi. 13, 14.

27. What ought we to take in our conflicts with foes? Eph. vi. 16, 17.

28. How did the proud Philistine receive the youthful champion of the Lord of hosts? 1 Sam. xvii. 42, 43.

29. What did the Philistine say to David? 1 Sam. xvii. 44.

30. In what noble language did David address his adversary? 1 Sam. xvii. 45.

31. How did David show his confidence in God? 1 Sam. xvii. 46, 47.

32. Upon what was the confidence based?

33. What proof did he receive that his trust in God was well founded? 1 Sam. xvii. 48–50.

34. What was the effect of his victory? 1 Sam. xvii. 51, 52.

35. What testimony did Saul give to the noble character of David? 1 Sam. xxiv. 16–18.

36. How can we obtain that confidence in God for which David was distinguished?

LESSON XXVII

DAVID, THE ILLUSTRIOUS MONARCH.

1. To whom did David go for direction after the death of Saul? 2 Sam. ii. 1.

2. Mention the names of other heroes who sought direction from God.

3. Where did David at first reside? 2 Sam. ii. 3

4. Where was Hebron situated?

5. What patriarchs lived and were buried there?

6. How old was David when he began to reign? 2 Sam. v. 4.

7. How long did he reign in Hebron over Judah? 2 Sam. v. 5, f. c.

8. How long did he reign in Jerusalem? 2 Sam v. 5, l. c.
9. What part of Jerusalem is called the "city of David"? 2 Sam. ii. 7, 9.
10. To what other place is this title given? Luke ii. 4.
11. By whom was David sustained in his battles with the Philistines? 2 Sam. v. 19.
12. How did David show his reverence for the ark of God? 2 Sam. vi. 1, 2, 17.
13. What pious purpose entered into his heart? 1 Kings viii. 17.
14. What had God done for David? 2 Sam. vii. 8, 9.
15. What promises did God make to him? 2 Sam. vii. 12, 13.
16. How did David manifest his piety? 2 Sam vii. 22, 26.
17. Upon what principles was the administration of David based? 2 Sam. viii. 15.
18. What were David's qualities as a writer?
19. What can you say of the beauties of the Psalms of David?
20. What can you say of their sublimity?
21. What historical events are recorded in the Psalms?
22. What references are made to the coming Messiah?
23. What is the character of the descriptions given of the Almighty Being?
24. Did David live without sin? Ps. li. 4.
25. What did he do after he had sinned? Ps. li. 1–3.
26. What would be his safeguard against sin in the future? Ps. li. 10–12.
27 What does God desire when we transgress? Ps. li. 16, 17

28. Did David live without trials? 2 Sam. xii. 15-19.

29. What consoled him? 2 Sam. xii. 20-23.

30. What other great trial befell him? 2 Sam. xviii. 33.

31. What preparations did David make for building a house to the Lord? 1 Chron. xxix. 2-5.

32. What gave to David great joy? 1 Chron xxix. 6-9.

33. What prayer did he offer up for his son Solomon? 1 Chron. xxix. 19.

34. What is said of David's death? 1 Chron xxix. 28.

35. What had been his experience in life? Ps ciii. 8-17.

LESSON XXVIII.

SOLOMON, THE KING, IN HIS GLORY.

1. Whom did David swear should succeed him on the throne? 1 Kings i. 29, 30.

2. What is the meaning of Solomon?

3. How long before Christ was he born?

4. What solemn charge did his father, the king, give to him? 1 Kings ii. 1-4.

5. How old was he when he received the throne? *Ans.* Eighteen years.

6. What did the prophet Nathan call him? 2 Sam xii. 25.

7. What is the meaning of Jedidiah?

8. Who tried to usurp the throne? 1 Kings i. 18, 19.

9. What means were adopted to defeat the plans of Adonijah? 1 Kings i. 32–35.

10. How did the people receive Solomon? 1 Kings i. 39.

11. How was Adonijah affected? 1 Kings i. 50.

12. How did Solomon deal with his rival? 1 Kings i. 51–53.

13. What promise had been made in connection with Solomon? 1 Chron. xxii. 9.

14. What did God say to him in a dream? 1 Kings iii. 5.

15. What did Solomon ask for? 1 Kings iii. 6–9.

16. What did God say to him? 1 Kings iii. 11, 12.

17. What did he promise to give to him? 1 Kings iii. 13.

18. What will God give to us if we ask him?

19. What principles must enter into our requests?

20. How did Solomon display his wisdom? 1 Kings iii. 16–27.

21. How were the people affected by this? 1 Kings iii. 28.

22. How large was Solomon's kingdom? 1 Kings iv. 21, 24.

23. What was the condition of the people? 1 Kings iv. 25.

24. Give some of the proofs of his great prosperity. 1 Kings iv. 26, 27; x. 14, 15, 23.

25. In what consisted Solomon's greatest glory? 1 Kings iv. 29, 30.

26. How extensive were his writings? 1 Kings iv 32, 33.

27. How many of his writings have been preserved?

28. What queen came to test his wisdom? 1 Kings x. 1.

29. Describe her interview with the king. 1 Kings x. 2, 3.

30. How was she impressed by his wisdom and the splendor of his kingdom? 1 Kings x. 4–7.

31. How did she express her feelings? 1 Kings x. 8, 9.

32. What gifts passed between them? 1 Kings x. 10–13.

33. Hath a greater than Solomon appeared on the earth?

34. What should we give to the Messiah, the King of kings?

35. How should we welcome him? Ps. xlv. 3–7; xlvii. 6–8.

36. How will he receive us if we serve him? Matt. xxv. 34.

LESSON XXIX.

SOLOMON, THE BUILDER OF THE TEMPLE OF GOD.

1. What special reasons were there why Solomon should build this temple? 1 Kings v. 4.

2. What preparations had David made for the work? 1 Chron. xxii. 2–4; xxix. 2–5.

3. What was to be the character of the edifice? 1 Chron. xxii. 5.

4. Why was not David permitted to build it? 1 Chron. xxii. 7, 8.

5. Whom did David command to assist Solomon? 1 Chron. xxii. 17–19.

6. What did David give to Solomon? 1 Chron. xxviii. 11–19.

7. How did David encourage Solomon? 1 Chron. xxviii. 20.

8. What was his design in building the temple? 2 Chron. ii. 4.

9. What were his views of the majesty and greatness of God? 2 Chron. ii. 5, 6.

10. What arrangements did Solomon make with Hiram, King of Tyre? 1 Kings v. 5-12.

11. How many men were employed in the work? 1 Kings v. 13-18.

12. How many years was this before Christ?

13. Will you describe the temple? 1 Kings vi. 14-22.

14. What promise did the Lord make in connection with it? 1 Kings viii. 13.

15. What was the appearance of the house of the Lord when completed?

16. Upon what mount was it built?

17. What preparations were made for the dedication of the temple? 1 Kings viii. 1, 2.

18. What did the priests bring up on this solemn occasion? 1 Kings viii. 3, 4.

19. What is the ark of the covenant?

20. How was it constructed?

21. What did it contain?

22. With what feelings was it regarded by the people?

23. Where was it placed? 1 Kings viii. 6.

24. What filled the house of the Lord? 1 Kings viii. 10, 11.

25. What was done before the ark? 1 Kings viii. 5

26. What did Solomon say on the occasion? 1 Kings viii. 12-21.

27. What beautiful prayer did he offer up? 1 Kings viii. 22, etc.

28. What blessing did he pronounce upon the people? 1 Kings viii. 55-61.

29. What other rites and festivities followed? 1 Kings viii. 62-65.

30. How were the people affected? 1 Kings viii 66.

31. Did God accept the dedication made to him? 1 Kings ix. 3.

32. What are the true temples of the living God?

33. How should we keep these temples?

LESSON XXX.

SOLOMON. — THE GLORY OBSCURED.

1. What peculiarities distinguish the biographies found in the sacred Scriptures?

2. Is there any attempt made to cover up the defects of great men?

3. What characters among those already considered are the purest?

4. Did the wisdom, good resolutions, prosperity, and glory of Solomon save him from sin? 1 Kings xi. 1.

5. Will our knowledge and resolutions save us from sin?

6. What will keep us from breaking God's laws?

7. How was Solomon's heart led away from God? 1 Kings xi. 4.

8. Why was his sin so great and aggravating? Neh. xiii. 26.

9. How deep was his fall? 1 Kings xi. 5, 6.

10. What was the builder of God's temple led away by sin to build? 1 Kings xi. 7, 8.

11. How do you account for such glaring apostasy?

12. How did God feel toward him? 1 Kings xi. 9.

13. What did God threaten to do? 1 Kings xi. 11.

14. What led God to mitigate the sentence against Solomon? 1 Kings xi. 13.

15. What shows God's infinite mercy? Ps. lxxxix. 33.

16. What promise had been made to David? Ps. lxxxix. 35–37.
17. What enemies were raised up against Solomon? 1 Kings xi. 14, 23, 26.
18. Why were these enemies stirred up?
19. In what respects was his glory obscured?
20. How long did Solomon reign? 1 Kings xi. 42.
21. How old was he when he died?
22. Who reigned in his stead? 1 Kings xi. 43.
23. What was Solomon's experience of the world? Eccl. i. 12–18.
24. At what period of his life did he write the book of Ecclesiastes?
25. What is the meaning of Ecclesiastes? Eccl. i. 1.
26. Is there evidence that Solomon repented of his awful sins?
27. How did he view worldly pleasures in his old age? Eccl. i. 2.
28. How can we avoid his errors and calamities? Prov. iv. 5, 6.
29. With what urgency is wisdom pressed upon us? Prov. iv. 7–9.
30. Against what are we warned by the example of Solomon?

LESSON XXXI.

ELIJAH. THE BOLD AND EARNEST PROPHET.

1 Who were the most distinguished prophets under the ancient dispensation?
2. Who afterward combined in his person the offices of prophet, priest, and king?

3. Why are there not prophets in our day?

4. How is Elijah introduced to our notice? 1 Kings xvii. 1.

5. At what period of the world was this?

6. What do we know of Elijah's early history?

7. How did God provide for him? 1 Kings xvii. 2-6.

8. How was he provided for when the waters of the brook failed? 1 Kings xvii. 7-15.

9. Why was the brook allowed to dry up?

10. Was the word of the Lord, as spoken by Elijah, true? 1 Kings xvii. 16.

11. What enabled Elijah to speak with such absolute confidence?

12. How did Elijah prove the power of prayer? 1 Kings xvii. 17-23.

13. Can such a power as this be exerted in our day? John xv. 7; xiv. 13, 14; Matt. xxi. 21, 22.

14. How long did the famine continue? Luke iv. 25.

15. What command came to Elijah the third year? 1 Kings xviii. 1.

16. What showed the boldness of the prophet? 1 Kings xviii. 8, 15, 16.

17. What did Ahab say to Elijah? 1 Kings xviii. 17.

18. What did he mean by this question?

19. What did Elijah reply?

20. When God comes out in judgment upon a nation for its sins, upon whom do wicked men cast the blame?

21. What is the true cause of the calamities?

22. For whom did Elijah ask Ahab to send? 1 Kings xviii. 19, 20.

23. What did he say to the people? 1 Kings xviii. 21.

24. What proposition did he make to them? 1 Kings xviii. 22-24.

25. What success did the prophets of Baal meet with? 1 Kings xviii. 26.
26. How did Elijah treat them? 1 Kings xviii. 27.
27. Did their great efforts avail anything? 1 Kings xviii. 28, 29.
28. What preparations did Elijah make? 1 Kings xviii. 30–35.
29. Upon what did Elijah rely for success? 1 Kings xviii. 36, 37.
30. Did God hear his prayer? 1 Kings xviii. 38.
31. What impression was made upon the people? 1 Kings xviii. 39.
32. Who sought Elijah's life? 1 Kings xix. 1, 2.
33. What feeling took possession of the prophet? 1 Kings xix. 4.
34. What produced his great sadness?
35. Did the Lord provide for him? 1 Kings xix. 5–8.
36. Did God again communicate with his servant? 1 Kings xix. 9–18.
37. How was Elijah rewarded for his heroic conduct and ardent piety? 2 Kings ii. 11.
38. How was he subsequently honored? Luke ix 30, 31.
39. Who was translated to heaven before him?

LESSON XXXII.

ELISHA, GOD'S CHOSEN PROPHET.

1. What were the special duties of the ancient prophets of God?
2. What proofs did they give that they spoke and acted under divine authority?

3 What character was it necessary for them to maintain, in order to hold the prophetic office?

4. By whom was Elisha called to be a prophet? 1 Kings xix. 15, 16.

5. What did Elijah cast upon him when they met? 1 Kings xix. 19.

6. Why did he cast his mantle upon him?

7. What was the prophet's mantle made of? Consult Heb. xi. 37.

8. What did Elisha do to show that he renounced the world and all temporal interests? 1 Kings xix. 21.

9. What advantages did Elisha enjoy, to prepare him for the prophetic office? 2 Kings ii. 2, 4, 6.

10. What request did he make of Elijah? 2 Kings ii. 9.

11. Was this request granted? 2 Kings ii. 10, 11.

12. What is meant by the "chariot of fire and horses of fire"?

13. What exclamation did Elisha utter when he saw Elijah translated to heaven? 2 Kings ii. 12.

14. Why did he call Elijah "my father"?

15. What did he mean by "the chariot of Israel and the horsemen thereof"?

16. What did Elisha take up? 2 Kings ii. 13.

17. What did Elisha do with the mantle? 2 Kings ii. 14.

18. Was the power in the mantle, or in Elisha, or in God?

19. By whom was Elisha mocked? 2 Kings ii. 23.

20. What punishment was inflicted upon these children? 2 Kings ii. 24.

21. Wherein consisted the greatness of their sin?

22. What proof did Elisha furnish that God was with him? 2 Kings ii. 21, 22; iv. 32–35, 41.

23. What effect did the miracles wrought by God's prophets have upon the people?

24 Whom did Elisha cure of leprosy? 2 Kings v. 9, 10, 14.

25. What danger threatened Elisha? 2 Kings vi. 13–15.

26. Did he fear the Syrian army? 2 Kings vi. 16.

27. What did he mean by saying "they that be with us are more than they that be with them"? Ps. lv. 18.

28. Need we fear anything if God is on our side? Rom. viii. 31.

29. How many years did Elisha prophesy?

30. When did he die? 2 Kings xiii. 14, 20.

31. Who lamented his death?

32. What lessons do we learn from the life of this prophet?

LESSON XXXIII.

ISAIAH, THE SUBLIME HEBREW POET AND PROPHET.

1. What prophets followed Elisha? *Ans.* Jonah, Amos, and Hosea.

2. During what periods did they prophesy? *Ans.* Jonah, 856–784 B. C. Amos, 810–785 B. C. Hosea, 810–725 B. C.

3. Who was Isaiah? Is. i. 1.

4. Under what kings did he prophesy? Is. i. 1.

5. During what periods did he prophesy? *Ans.* From about 760 to 707 B. C.

6. By what other name was he called? Matt. iii. 3.

7. What is the meaning of Isaiah?

8. In what city did he reside?

9. What rank did these prophets hold in Judea?

10 What was the character of Isaiah?

11. How did he rank in relation to the other prophets?

12. What was the condition of Judah at the time he lived? Is. i. 4–9.

13. What language did he address to the people? Is. i. 10–15.

14. What, in God's name, does he require of the people? Is. i. 16, 17.

15. How does he express the great mercy of God? Is. i. 18.

16. Under what parable does he present what God had done for Judah? Is. v. 1–4.

17. What punishment was threatened? Is. v. 5–7.

18. Against what classes of sinners does he utter woes? Is. v. 8, 11, 20–24.

19. In what language of startling sublimity does he describe the mustering of the hosts against Babylon? Is. xiii. 1–5.

20. How does he describe the destruction of Babylon? Is. xiii. 19–22.

21. Have these prophecies been literally fulfilled?

22. What proofs have we of the inspiration of the writings of these prophets?

23. What is said of Moab? Is. xv. 1–3.

24. What is foretold of Damascus? Is. xvii. 1–3.

25. What judgments are threatened against the Ethiopians? Is. xviii. 1–6.

26. What is foretold concerning the Egyptians? Is. xix. 1–4.

27. What does Isaiah prophesy against Jerusalem? Is. xxii. 1–7.

28. Why does he predict these terrible calamities? Is. l. 1–5; xxiv. 5, 6.

29. Under whose authority did he act? Is. vi. 9, 10.

30. What glorious vision did he have of the Lord? Is vi. 1–4.

31. By whom was he prepared for his great work? Is. vi. 5–7.

32. Does Isaiah foretell the Babylonian captivity? Is. xxxix. 3–8.

33. Does he predict the future deliverance of Israel? Is. xxv. 1–8; xxvi. 1–4.

34. What may be said of the beauty of this song?

35. To what period does it apply?

36. How long before the people were carried away captives to Babylon was this written? *Ans.* About 124 years.

37. How long before their restoration to their own country was it written?

38. What can you say of the peculiarities of Isaiah's style of writing?

LESSON XXXIV.

ISAIAH, THE EVANGELICAL PROPHET.

1. Why is Isaiah called the evangelical prophet?

2. What does Jerome say of him? *Ans.* He says, "He has so clearly explained the whole mystery of Christ and the church that you will regard him, not as predicting future events, but as composing a history of the past."

3. After surveying the sins and sufferings of the Jews, to what bright and happy days does the prophet turn his eye? Is. ii. 1–4.

4. Under whose advent will these blessings be enjoyed? Is. ii. 5; John i. 4, 9; viii. 12.

5. Where does a similar prophecy occur? Micah iv. 1–5.

6. What portion of the book of Isaiah specially relates to the coming of Christ? *Ans.* From the fortieth chapter to the end of the book.

7. What can you say of this part of the Old Testament? *Ans.* It is the most sublime, rich, and important part of the Old Testament, and will deeply interest the thoughtful and virtuous, in all ages of the world.

8. Why do you say this? *Ans.* Because Isaiah here treats of the coming of Christ, his divine nature, and exalted work; his instructions, trials, and victories; the manner of his life, his death, and the happiness and glory that will follow his advent.

9. Does any other prophet linger with such minuteness and delight upon these themes?

10. What glad tidings does Isaiah bring to the people? Is. xl. 1–2.

11. Where is the scene of this vision laid?

12. What voice heralds the deliverance from Babylon, and the coming of the Messiah? Is. xl. 3–5.

13. What other prophecy refers to the forerunner of Christ? Mal. iii. 1.

14. To whom are these passages applied? Matt. iii. 1-3

15. What beautiful description is given of the Messiah? Is. xlii. 1–4.

16. How do you know that these words apply to Christ? Matt. xii. 17–21.

17. What is said of his work? Is. xlii. 7; xxxv. 5, 6.

18. Prove that these words apply to Christ? Matt. xi. 5; xii. 22; xx. 30, etc.

19. How are the sufferings of the Saviour described? Is. liii. 3–5.

20 Was this prophecy fulfilled? Matt. viii. 17; Heb. ix. 28.

21. How is the office of the Messiah described? Is. lxi. 1–3.

22. Prove that these words refer to Jesus our great Redeemer? Luke iv. 18–21.

23. What is said of the glorious results of his coming? Is. lxi. 4–6, 9–11.

24. How are the triumphs of the Messiah celebrated? Is. lxiii. 1–6. Rev. xix. 15, 16.

25. How are the last days and death of Christ described? Is. liii. 7, 8.

26. Were these words fulfilled? Matt. xxvi.; 63, xxvii. 12, 14.

27. What is said of his burial? Is. liii. 9.

28. How was this declaration fulfilled? Matt. xxvii. 57, 58, 60.

29. Ought we not to cordially believe in such a Prophet and such a Saviour?

30. Give your reasons in full, for such a belief.

31. What account can you give of the death of Isaiah? *Ans.* The Jews and early fathers say that he was put to death by Manasseh, by being sawn asunder.

LESSON XXXV.

JEREMIAH, THE MESSENGER OF JEHOVAH'S WRATH.

1. At what period did Jeremiah prophesy? Jer. i. 1–3.

2. What divine purpose was fulfilled in his career? Jer. i. 5.

3. How early did he prophesy? Jer. i. 6.

4. How did the Lord encourage him? Jer. i 7, 8.

5. From whom did Jeremiah receive his power? Jer. i. 9 10.

6. What is the general subject of his prophecies? Jer. i. 14–16.

7. What solemn command came to him? Jer. i. 17.

8. What is the duty of all men? Eph. vi. 14–17.

9. What does God say that he has made this prophet? Jer. i. 18.

10. What was the secret of his power? Jer. i. 19.

11. What were his feelings concerning Judah? Jer. iv. 19; xv. 5.

12. How does he describe the desolation that is to come upon the land? Jer. iv. 23–29.

13. How is the desperate wickedness of the people portrayed? Jer. v. 1–6; xxiii. 25–31.

14. How are the fearful judgments of the Almighty described? Jer. v. 14–17; vi. 19–23; vii. 32–34.

15. How were the threatenings carried into execution? Jer. xxxix. 1, 8, 9; lii. 12–15.

16. Does Jeremiah predict the coming of the Messiah? Jer. xxiii. 5, 6.

17. What does he predict as to the duration of the captivity in Babylon? Jer. xxv. 11.

18. What does he predict concerning Babylon? Jer. xxv. 12, 13; li. 1–3, 8, 9, 27, etc.

19. Against what other nations does he open the judgments of heaven? Jer. xxv. 15, 19–26.

20. What is said of Egypt? Jer. xlvi. 2, 8–12.

21. What is the word of the Lord against the Philistines? Jer. xlvii. 1–4.

22. What is said of Moab? Jer. xlviii. 1–6.

23. What is said of the Ammonites? Jer. xlix. 1–3.

24. Did this faithful prophet meet with persecution?

25. What conspiracy was formed against him? Jer. xi. 18, 19.

26. When was he imprisoned as a deserter? Jer. xxxvii. 11–15.
27. Who released him? Jer. xxxvii. 17.
28. Of what is he again accused? Jer. xxxviii 1–4.
29. What was done to him? Jer. xxxviii. 6.
30. How was he taken out of the dungeon? Jer xxxviii. 10–13.
31. How was he delivered out of the court of the prison? Jer. xxxix. 11–14.
32. Describe the character of Jeremiah.
33. What writings has he left.

LESSON XXXVI.

EZEKIEL, THE SEER OF VISIONS.

1. Who was Ezekiel? Ezek. i. 3.
2. At what period of the world did he live?
3. What great event took place in his time?
4. When were the Jews carried away captive to Babylon?
5. When did the visions of God open to him? Ezek. i. 1.
6. What first appeared to him? Ezek. i. 4–14.
7. What was the appearance of the wheels? Ezek i. 15–19.
8. What animated and moved them? Ezek. i 20–23.
9. As they went, what did he hear? Ezek. i. 24 25.

10 What did he see above the firmament? Ezek. i. 26-28.

11. What divine commission did he receive? Ezek. ii. 2, 3.

12. What spirit was he commanded to manifest? Ezek. ii. 6.

13. To whom had a similar command been given? Jer. i. 8, 17.

14. Against what was he warned? Ezek. ii. 8.

15. What did he see in vision? Ezek. ii. 9, 10; iii. 1-3.

16. Explain the vision of the eating of the roll.

17. To whom was the prophet sent. Ezek. iii. 4-6.

18. How was he to be sustained in his difficult and perilous undertaking? Ezek. iii. 8, 9.

19. How are his responsibilities set forth? Ezek. iii. 17-21.

20. How is the final desolation of Israel depicted? Ezek. vii. 3, 4, 8, 9.

21. What shall be the condition of the people? Ezek. vii. 16-18.

22. What will become of their treasures? Ezek. vii. 19.

23. Describe the vision of the coals of fire? Ezek. x. 1-7.

24. Describe the vision of the cherubim? Ezek. x. 8, etc.

25. Did Ezekiel have a vision of the restoration of the temple? Ezek. xl. 1; xli. 1.

26. What is said of the return of God's glory to the temple? Ezek. xliii. 1, 2, 5.

27. What promise does God make to his people? Ezek. xliii. 7-9.

28. Who will be excluded from the priesthood? Ezek. xliii. 9, 10.

29. Who will be permitted to minister before the Lord? Ezek. xliv. 15, 16

30. What are the peculiarities of the writings of the prophet Ezekiel?

NOTE. In these lessons on the prophets, it is impossible to bring within the limits of a single lesson anything more than a few general facts from their writings. It is to be hoped, however, that even this imperfect view will stimulate the student to a careful examination of the whole book of prophecy.

LESSON XXXVII.

DANIEL, THE GREAT PROPHET DURING THE CAPTIVITY.

1. For what purpose was Daniel raised up? *Ans.* To maintain the true religion among the captive Jews in Chaldea, and to utter the most magnificent and extensive prophecies ever delivered.
2. Give some account of his early history. Dan. i. 1–6.
3. Did he resist the temptations in the king's palace? Dan. i. 8–16.
4. To whom was he indebted for his wisdom and knowledge? Dan. i. 17.
5. Why was Daniel so highly gifted above his companions?
6. How was the king impressed by these young servants of the Lord? Dan. i. 20.
7. Whom did the king call, to make known to him his dream, with the interpretation thereof? Dan. ii. 1–6.
8. What did the king require? Dan. ii. 7–9.
9. What was the result of this interview. Dan. ii 10–13.

10. What course did Daniel take? Dan. ii. 16–18.

11. How did he obtain a knowledge of the secret? Dan. ii. 19.

12. How does he express his gratitude to God? Dan. ii. 23.

13. How does Daniel describe the dream? Dan. ii 31–35.

14. To what does the "head of fine gold" refer? Dan. ii. 37, 38.

15. To what nation does the breast and arms of silver refer? Dan. v. 28, 31.

16. What nation is presented under the type of "the belly and thighs of brass"? Dan. vii. 23.

17. What is the fourth nation referred to with "legs of iron"? Dan. ii. 40; vii. 7, 23.

18. What is the great spiritual kingdom referred to in Dan. ii. 34, 35? Dan. ii. 44; iv. 3; vii. 13, 14.

19. In what other vision do the four great empires appear to the prophet? Dan. vii. 1–7.

20. What fervent prayer does Daniel offer to God? Dan. ix. 16–19.

21. Who appeared to the prophet? Dan. ix. 21.

22. Who is Gabriel?

23. What did he say to Daniel? Dan. ix. 24.

24. What space of time is here represented by a week? Comp. Lev. xxv. 8; Ezek. iv. 6.

25. What period is here predicted? *Ans.* As a day in prophetic language is a year, we have, in this prediction, 490 years "from the commission given to Ezra to Christ's crucifixion, or 434 years from the completion of the second temple, *which was exactly fulfilled.*"

26. Were the other prophecies of Daniel fulfilled with equal exactness?

27. What did Porphyry, the bitter enemy of the Bible say? *Ans.* He said that such prophecies so

accurately fulfilled, must have been written before the event took place.

28. What should we say? Dan. ii. 20–22. 2 Peter i. 21

LESSON XXXVIII

EZRA, THE LEADER OF THE JEWISH NATION.

1. Who was Ezra?
2. What offices did he hold?
3. What was his character?
4. How many years does his narrative of Jewish history embrace?
5. What event does he first record? Ezra i. 1–3.
6. To what "word of the Lord, by the mouth of Jeremiah," does he here refer? Jer. xxv. 12; xxix. 10.
7. What prophecy is referred to in the words, "he hath charged us to build him a house at Jerusalem"? Is. xliv. 28; xlv. 1, 13.
8. Is it possible, for any amount of infidel labor to do away with such proofs as these of the divine authority of the Holy Scriptures?
9. What was the effect of the proclamation of King Cyrus? Ezra i. 5, 6.
10. What was done with the sacred vessels of the house of the Lord? Ezra i. 7–11.
11. How many persons returned to Jerusalem at this time? Ezra ii. 64, 65.
12. What religious rites and services were re-established? Ezra iii. 1–6.
13. When were the foundations of the temple laid? Ezra iii. 8–10.

14. When was the temple finished? Ezra vi. 15.

15. What services were performed at the dedication of the temple? Ezra vi. 16–18.

16. Under what king did Ezra go up to Jerusalem? Ezra vii. 1, 6.

17 Who went with him? Ezra vii. 7.

18 Who were the Nethinims?

19. What could they with propriety say? Ps lxxxiv. 10.

20. What language expresses the feelings of the holy and zealous Ezra. Ps. lxxxiv. 2, 11.

21. What were the objects that Ezra had in view in returning to Jerusalem?

22. What preparation did he make for his work? Ezra vii. 10; viii. 21.

23. What important aid did he receive from the king? Ezra vii. 11–20.

24. What favors were conferred upon him? Ezra vii. 21–23.

25. What civil authority did Ezra carry with him? Ezra vii. 25, 26.

26. How does Ezra express his gratitude? Ezra vii. 27, 28.

27. Give an account of the journey? Ezra viii. 24–32.

28. What was done after three days? Ezra viii. 33–36.

29. What sins did Ezra find prevailing in the holy city? Ezra ix. 1, 2.

30. How was he affected? Ezra ix. 3, 4.

31. What prayer did he offer to God? Ezra ix. 5, 6, etc.

32. What was the effect of his prayer and confessions? Ezra x. 1–5.

33. What proclamation was made? Ezra x. 7, 8.

34 How did he exhort the people? Ezra x. 9–11.

35. What was the effect of his labors? Ezra x. 12–17.

36. For what qualities was Ezra distinguished?

37. What is Ezra generally believed to have done in regard to the books of the Old Testament?

LESSON XXXIX.

NEHEMIAH, THE REFORMER IN JERUSALEM.

1. Who succeeded Ezra in the government of Jerusalem?
2. When and where was Nehemiah born?
3. Of what nation were his parents?
4. Why had they remained so long in Babylon?
5. What office did Nehemiah hold under the Persian king? Neh. i. 11, l. c.
6. What advantage did this office give to him?
7. What awakened his interest in the Jews in Jerusalem? Neh. i. 2, 3.
8. How was he affected by these sad accounts? Neh. i. 4.
9. What prayer and confession did he make to God? Neh. i. 5–11.
10. Describe his interview with the king? Neh. ii. 1–8.
11. How many years was this after Ezra went to Jerusalem?
12. How was Nehemiah attended on the journey? Neh. ii. 9.
13. Why were soldiers sent with him?
14. When did he survey the ruins of the city? Neh. ii. 12, 13.
15. What did he desire to do? Neh. ii. 17.
16. What did the people say? Neh. ii. 18.
17. Who laughed them to scorn? Neh. ii. 19.

18. What motives induced these men to oppose the rebuilding of the walls?

19. When did Sanballat and Tobiah again show their hostility? Neh. iv. 1–3.

20. Were the servants of God stopped in their work? Neh. iv. 6; vi. 15.

21. Give an account of the dedication of the wall Neh. xii. 27, etc.

22. To whom was the city given in charge? Neh vii. 1–4.

23. What efforts were made for the religious instruction of the people? Neh. viii. 1–3.

24. Were the people ready to receive instruction? Neh. viii. 13.

25. How did they keep the feast of tabernacles? Neh. viii. 16–18.

26. What offices were arranged for the temple? Neh. xii. 44–47.

27. What did Nehemiah do to the chambers of the temple? Neh. xiii. 4–9.

28. What abuses did he correct in the house of God? Neh. xiii. 10–13.

29. What reforms did he effect in regard to the Sabbath? Neh. xiii. 15–22.

30. What reformation did he make in regard to marriages? Neh. xiii. 23–25.

31. What striking example did he refer to? Neh. xiii. 26.

32. What arrangements did he finally make? Neh. xiii. 30, 31.

33. What historical books close with this book?

34. For what characteristics was Nehemiah distinguished?

LESSON XL.

JOHN THE BAPTIST, THE FORERUNNER OF JESUS CHRIST.

1. Upon what ancient custom was "the forerunner" founded?
2. What prophecy foretold the coming of John? Is. xl. 3.
3. How do we know that this applies to John the Baptist? Matt. iii. 3.
4. What other prophet foretold his coming? Mal. iii. 1.
5. Who were the parents of John? Luke i. 5.
6. What is the meaning "of the course of Abia"? 1 Chron. xxiii. 24; xxiv. 10, 19.
7. With whom does John rank by birth?
8. What was the character of his parents? Luke i. 6.
9. Who appeared to the holy priest? Luke i. 11.
10. What did the angel say to him? Luke i. 13, 14.
11. What did the angel say concerning John? Luke i. 15, 16.
12. The spirit and power of what prophet would be upon him? Luke i. 17.
13. Had this been before predicted? Mal. iv. 5, 6.
14. Was this fulfilled? Matt. xi. 14; Mark ix. 12, 13.
15. What angel appeared to Zacharias? Luke i. 19.
16. Had this angel appeared before on the earth? Dan. viii. 16; ix. 21.
17. What circumstances attended the naming of the child? Luke i. 59–66.

18 How did the father show his gratitude? Luke i. 67, 68.

19. What prophecies were fulfilled in the birth and mission of John? Luke i. 70, etc.

20. What is said of the early history of the child? Luke i. 80.

21. When did John begin to preach? Luke iii. 1, 2

22. What did he preach? Luke iii. 3. Matt. iii. 1, 2.

23. How was he dressed? Matt. iii. 4.

24. Why was he dressed so? Comp. 2 Kings i. 8; Zech. xiii. 4.

25. What was the effect of his preaching? Matt. iii. 5, 6.

26. What did he say to the Sadducees? Matt. iii. 7–9.

27. What kind of a reformer is he? Matt. iii. 10.

28. How does he refer to Christ? Matt. iii. 11; Mark i. 8.

29. Give an account of his baptizing Christ? Matt. iii. 13–17.

30. What prophecies were at this time fulfilled? Is. xi. 2; xlii. 1.

31. What was the object of John's mission? John i. 6–8.

32. What witness did John bare? John i. 15.

33. What did John say when he saw Jesus? John i. 29–31.

34. What record did he bare? John i. 32–34.

35. What persecution did he suffer? Luke iii. 19, 20; Mark vi. 17–19.

36. Give an account of his death and burial? Matt. xiv. 6–12.

37. What did Christ say of him? Matt. xi. 11.

38. For what characteristics was John the Baptist distinguished?

LESSON XLI.

JESUS CHRIST, THE PROMISED MESSIAH.

1 What is a prophecy?

2 By what power were the ancient prophets enabled to predict future events? 2 Peter i. 21; 1 Cor. xii. 10, 11.

3. Did Christ appeal to the prophecies concerning himself? Luke xviii. 31; xxiv. 44.

4. Did the Jews believe that the Old Testament contained prophecies respecting the Messiah? Matt. ii. 4–6.

5. Where do we find recorded the first intimation of a coming Messiah? Gen. iii. 15.

6. Who is meant by the seed of the woman? Gal. iv. 4, 5.

7. In what manner was he to bruise the serpent's head? Heb. ii. 14; 1 John iii. 8, l. c.

8. What prediction is given in Is. vii. 14?

9. What is the meaning of Immanuel? Matt. i. 23.

10. Was the place of Christ's birth predicted? Micah v. 2.

11. Was this fulfilled? Matt. ii. 1.

12. What prophecy was uttered respecting the miracles of Christ? Is. xxxv. 5, 6.

13. Was this prophecy fulfilled? Matt. xv. 30.

14. What promises were given that they should receive the Spirit of the Lord? Is. xi. 2; lxi. 1.

15. Were these promises fulfilled? Matt. iii. 16 John i. 33; iii. 34.

16. What was said in regard to the treatment that Christ should receive? Is. liii. 2, 3.

17. Did these words prove to be true? John i. 11. Luke xix 14; Matt. xxvii. 23

18 Were his personal sufferings foretold? Is. liii. 4, 5.

19. Prove that this language was fulfilled. Matt. viii. 20; Luke xxii. 42.

20. What important prediction did Moses utter? Deut. xviii. 15–18.

21. To whom did St. Peter apply this prediction? Acts iii. 19–24.

22. What proof is there that the Saviour applied the words of Moses to himself? John v. 46.

23. What prophecies were uttered respecting the persecution of the Messiah? Ps. lxix. 26; Is. liii. 4.

24. Were these fulfilled? John v. 16, 18; xv. 20.

25. What prophecy do you find in regard to the selling of Christ for money? Zech. xi. 12.

26. Was this accurately fulfilled? Matt. xxvi. 15.

27. How was it foretold that the money should be disposed of? Zech. xi. 13.

28. How was it actually applied? Matt. xxvii. 7, 8.

29. What was said respecting his silence? Isa. liii. 7. Fulfilled Matt. xxvii. 12; I Peter ii. 23.

30. What is said about parting his garments? Ps. xxii. 18. Fulfilled Mark xv. 24.

31. What was said about his burial? Isa. liii. 9. Fulfilled Matt. xxvii. 57–60.

32. What about his resurrection? Ps. xvi. 10. Fulfilled Matt. xxviii. 5–7.

33. Can we ask for stronger proof than is here furnished that Jesus Christ is the promised Messiah?

LESSON XLII.

JESUS CHRIST, THE SON OF GOD.

1. What exalted titles are given to Christ by Isaiah? Is. ix. 6; vii. 14.
2. How does David present him to us? Ps. ii. 7.
3. What voice was heard from heaven? Matt. iii. 17
4. What was the testimony of John the Baptist? John i. 34.
5. What did Paul preach? Acts ix. 20; Rom. i. 4
6. What is said of the glory of Christ? John xvii. 5.
7. Who witnessed his glory? John i. 14; 2 Peter i. 17.
8. Should Christ be worshipped? John v. 23.
9. Was he worshipped on earth? Matt. ii. 2, Luke xxiv. 52.
10. Is Christ worshipped now? Rev. v. 13.
11. Is he called in the Scriptures God? John i. 1; Rom. ix. 5; 1 Tim. iii. 16; Heb. i. 8.
12. What proof is there of Christ's divine power? John i. 3; Col. i. 16, 17.
13. How will he manifest his power in the future? John v. 25, 28, 29.
14. What is a miracle?
15. What other terms are used in the Scriptures to designate miracles?
16. Why are they called signs? Mark xvi. 20; Heb. ii. 4.
17. Why are they called wonders? Mark ii. 12; Acts iii. 10, 11.
18. Describe the first miracle that Christ performed? John ii. 6–10.
19 Why was this miracle wrought? John ii. 11.

20. How did it manifest his glory?

21. How did it prove that he possessed almighty power?

22. Had Christ power over the natural world? Luke v. 4–7.

23. Give another instance of his power? Matt. viii. 23–27.

24. Give an example of Christ's creative power. Matt. xiv. 15–20.

25. How many witnesses were there of this great miracle? Matt. xiv. 21.

26. Did Christ have power over the diseases of the human body? Matt. iv. 23, 24.

27. Was there any malady that he could not cure? Matt. xv. 30.

28. Had he power over evil spirits? Matt. viii. 16, 28–32.

29. Had he power over death? Matt. ix. 25; Luke vii. 11–15; John xi. 39–44.

30. What miracles accompanied the death of Christ? Matt. xxvii. 45, 51, 52.

31. What was the testimony of the centurion and others? Matt. xxvii. 54.

LESSON XLIII.

JESUS CHRIST, THE GREAT TEACHER.

1. What was one of the great duties that Christ came to perform? Luke iv. 43.

2. Where did he preach? Luke iv. 44

3. Did Jesus preach also in other places? Luke v. 1, 3; Matt v. 1.

4. What did he teach concerning himself? John xiv. 6.

5. What is meant by Christ being "the way"? Heb. ix. 8, 12.

6. In what sense was he "the truth"? John i. 17; viii. 32.

7. In what sense was he "the life"? John xi. 25, 26.

8. In what sense will the believer never die?

9. What new commandment did Christ give? John xiii. 34.

10. How would men know that they were his disciples? John xiii. 35.

11. Why are we taught to believe in Christ? John xiv. 1.

12. What is the force of this argument?

13. What does Christ teach concerning the future life? John xiv. 2, 3.

14. What does he teach concerning the power of faith in him? John xiv. 12.

15. What is the meaning of the passage, "greater works than these shall he do"?

16. What promises does he give in connection with prayer? John xiv. 13, 14.

17. Is this language to be understood literally? Matt. vii. 7; xxi. 22.

18. What other promises does he make? Mark xi. 24; John xv. 7, 16; xvi. 23, 24.

19. Why does Jesus say so much about prayer?

20. What does he teach concerning the union between himself and his disciples? John xv. 4.

21. Who will bring forth fruit? John xv. 5.

22. How is the Father glorified? John xv. 8.

23. What is the test of our love for Christ? John xiv. 15; xv. 10.

24. What commandment does Christ repeat? John xiii. 34; xv. 12, 17.

25. Why does he so often repeat it?

26. What does Christ call his disciples? John xv. 15.

27. What promise does he make in regard to the Comforter? John xiv. 16, 17.

28. What will the Holy Ghost teach them? John xiv. 26.

29. What did Christ say of himself before Pilate? John xviii. 37.

30. What was his last command? Matt. xxviii 18, 19.

31. What were the disciples to teach? Matt xxviii. 20.

LESSON XLIV.

JESUS CHRIST, THE SAVIOUR OF THE WORLD

1. Why did Christ come into the world? 1 Tim i. 15.

2. How many is he able to save? Heb. vii. 25.

3. How are we saved? Eph. ii. 8; Acts xv. 11.

4. What must we do to be saved? Acts xiv. 31; Rom. x. 9.

5. Can we be saved in any other way than through Christ? Acts iv. 12; Heb. ii. 3.

6. To whom is Christ the author of salvation? Heb. v. 9.

7. Under what other title was Christ promised? Is. lix. 20.

8. Did he come as a redeemer? Titus ii. 14.

9. With what did he redeem us? 1 Peter i. 18; Rev. v. 9.

10. From what has he redeemed us? Gal. iii. 13.

11. By what other title is he known? 1 Tim. ii. 5.

12. Of what is Christ the mediator? Heb. viii. 6; ix. 15.

13. What is this new covenant? Heb. viii. 8--11.

14. By what other title is Christ known? Heb ix. 11.

15. How does he enter the holy place? Heb. ix. 12.

16. Why was Christ offered as a sacrifice? Heb. ix. 28; x. 14.

17. How may we enter "the holiest"? Heb. x. 19, 20.

18. How should we draw near to God? Heb. x 21, 22.

19. Why should we hold fast our profession? Heb. x. 23.

20. What will be the consequence of sinning wilfully, after having received the knowledge of the truth? Heb. x. 26, 27.

21. Under what other form is the great salvation by Christ presented? Rom. v. 10.

22. How are we justified through Christ? Rom v. 18, 19.

23. How are we sanctified? 1 Cor. vi. 11; Eph. v. 25.

24. How are we saved? Titus iii. 5, 6.

25. Being justified by his grace, what do we become? Titus iii. 7.

26. We are made heirs of what? 1 John ii. 25; v. 11.

27. What will the King say to those on his right hand? Matt. xxv. 34.

28. What will he say to those on the left hand? Matt. xxv. 41.

29. What will be the final destiny of the human race? Matt. xxv. 46.

30. What is our duty, in view of the future? 2 Peter iii. 14, 18.

LESSON XLV.

ST. PETER, THE PRINCE OF THE APOSTLES.

1. Why was St. Peter called the prince of the apostles?
2. For what mental qualities was he distinguished?
3. What were his moral characteristics?
4. What proof is there of his boldness?
5. Was he ever rash or presumptuous?
6. Did he always withstand temptation?
7. Of what country was Peter? Matt. iv. 18.
8. What was his employment in early life?
9. What advantages had he for obtaining an education?
10. What did Christ say that he would make of him? Matt. iv. 19.
11. What did he mean by this?
12. Who first told Peter of the Messiah? John i. 41.
13. What did Christ say that he should be called? John i. 42.
14. What did Peter say of Christ? Matt. xvi. 16.
15. Who revealed this to him? Matt. xvi. 17.
16. What did Christ then say? Matt. xvi. 18.
17. What did he say that he would give him? Matt. xvi. 19.
18. How do you explain this verse?
19. What miracle did Christ perform in Peter's house? Luke iv. 38, 39.
20. What miracle did Peter witness by the Lake of Gennesaret? Luke v. 3–7.
21. How was Peter affected by it? Luke v. 8.
22. What commission did Peter receive with the other apostles? Matt. x. 5–7.

23. What power was conferred upon him? Matt x. 8.

24. Had Peter any authority over the other apostles? *Ans.* There is not the least evidence that he had.

25. What gave him influence?

26. How were the disciples affected, seeing Jesus walking on the sea? Matt. xiv. 26.

27. What did Jesus say to them? Matt. xiv. 27.

28. What did Peter then say? Matt. xiv. 28.

29. What was the consequence of his experiment? Matt. xiv. 29–31.

30. Was Peter strongly attached to Christ? Matt. xxvi. 33 ; John xviii. 10.

31. What did Christ prophesy concerning him? Matt. xxvi. 34.

32. What did Peter then say? Matt. xxvi. 35.

33. Did Peter keep his good resolution? Matt. xxvi. 69–74.

34. How was he affected when he remembered the words of Jesus? Matt. xxvi. 75.

35. Was Peter sincere in his resolution to stand up for Jesus?

36. What led to his fall?

37. What does Christ say to us? Mark xiii. 37.

LESSON XLVI.

ST. PETER, THE FIRST GREAT PREACHER OF THE GOSPEL.

1. Did Peter lose his faith in Christ by the crucifixion and burial of his Lord?

2. How was he affected by the rumor that Christ had risen from the dead? Luke xxiv. 12.

3. When did Christ appear to his disciples after his resurrection? John xx. 19, 26.

4. When did he appear again? John xxi. 1, 2, 4.

5. What conversation took place between Jesus and Peter? John xxi. 15–17.

6. Why did Christ repeat the question three times?

7. To what divine attribute in Christ does Peter testify? John xxi. 17.

8. What does Christ prophesy concerning Peter? John xxi. 18.

9. What is meant by this language? John xxi. 19.

10. Did Peter remember this? 2 Peter i. 14.

11. What did Peter do after the ascension of Christ? Acts i. 13, 14.

12. What address did he make concerning Judas? Acts i. 15–22.

13. What followed the address? Acts i. 23–26.

14. Who opened before the people "the glorious gospel of the blessed God"? Acts ii. 14.

15. What charge does he refute? Acts. ii. 15.

16. What prophecies does he quote? Acts ii. 16–21.

17. What bold charge does he bring against the people? Acts ii. 22–24.

18. What does he quote from David? Acts ii. 25–28.

19. How does he conclude his discourse? Acts ii 29–36.

20. How were the people affected? Acts ii. 37.

21. What did Peter then say to them? Acts ii. 38–40.

22. What were the fruits from the precious seed of divine truth? Acts ii. 41, 42.

23. What striking miracle did Peter perform? Acts iii. 1–8.

24. How were the people affected by it? Acts iii. 10.

25 What bold and stirring address did Peter then make to the people? Acts iii. 12–18.

26. What did he exhort them to do? Acts iii. 19, etc.

27. Was Peter persecuted? Acts iv. 1–3.

28. What address did he make to the rulers? Acts iv. 8–12.

29. How were the rulers affected? Acts viii. 13.

30. What were Peter and John commanded not to do? Acts iv. 18.

31. Did they obey? Acts iv. 19, 20.

32. What awful calamity came through the agency of Peter upon Ananias and Sapphira? Acts v. 1–10.

33. Were the apostles again imprisoned? Acts v 17, 18.

34. By whom were they released? Acts v. 19.

35. What vision appeared to Peter? Acts x. 9–18.

36. How did Peter preach before Cornelius? Acts x. 34–43.

37. What was the effect of his discourse? Acts x. 44–48.

38. What question came before the apostles and elders? Acts xv. 1–5.

39. What did Peter say? Acts xv. 6–11.

40. Give an account of the death of St. Peter.

LESSON XLVII.

ST. JOHN, THE BELOVED DISCIPLE.

1. Why is St. John called the beloved disciple?
2. Wherein did he differ from St. Peter?
3. What can you say of his meditative spirit?
4. What can you say of his spirituality?

5. Give some account of his early history. Matt iv. 21, 22; Luke v. 10.

6. How did John early show his decision of character? Luke v. 11.

7. How intimate were his relations to Christ?

8. With what other eminent apostles was he often associated? Luke ix. 28.

9. What change did he witness in Christ while he prayed? Luke ix. 29.

10. Who appeared in glory to him? Luke ix. 30, 31.

11. What voice was heard? Luke ix. 35.

12. How did John display the vigor and fearlessness of his character? Luke ix. 51–54.

13. On what other occasion did he show these qualities? John xviii. 15.

14. Did he surpass even Peter in these qualities? John xviii. 16

15. What was John surnamed? Mark iii. 17.

16. On what occasion did John and James show an ambitious spirit? Mark x. 35–37.

17. How did Jesus reply to them? Mark x. 38.

18. What did they say? Mark x. 39, f. c.

19. What did Jesus then say? Mark x. 39, 40.

20. What important advice did Jesus then give? Mark x. 42–45.

21. What commission was given to John? Luke xxii. 8.

22. What other token of affection did John receive from Christ? John xiii. 23.

23. What scene of agony did John witness? Mark xiv. 33–36.

24. What advice did he receive from his Master? Mark xiv. 38.

25. Was John an eye-witness of the arrest of Jesus? John xviii. 1–13.

26. Did he witness the trial of Christ? John xviii. 15, etc.

27. Did he witness the crucifixion? John xix. 1, etc.

28. Whom did Jesus commit to the care of John? John xix. 26, 27.

29. Which of the Saviour's virtues did John reflect in his character?

30. What do you see in the life of St. John, as thus far considered, to imitate?

LESSON XLVIII.

ST. JOHN, THE EVER-FAITHFUL APOSTLE.

1. Did John see Christ after his resurrection? John xx. 19, 20.

2. Did he witness the ascension? Luke xxiv. 50, 51.

3. Where did John reside after this event? Luke xxiv. 52.

4. With whom was he associated in working miracles and preaching the gospel? Acts iii. 1.

5. Did he suffer persecution? Acts iv. 1–3.

6. Was he a successful preacher? Acts iv. 4.

7. What was the secret of his power? Acts iv. 13, l. c.

8. What was he commanded not to do? Acts iv. 18.

9. Did he obey God or man? Acts iv. 19, 20.

10. What was John in the church? Gal. ii. 9.

11. Whither did he remove about A. D. 65? *Ans.* It is supposed that he removed to Ephesus, and labored to extend the gospel in Asia Minor.

12. To what island was he banished, probably by Domitian?

13. To what age did he live? *Ans.* Ninety-four.

14. What year did he die? *Ans.* A. D. 100.

15. What had he seen of the progress of Christianity?

16. Did he outlive all the other apostles?

17. Mention the most striking events that occurred during his life.

18. What writings has he left?

19. What are some of the peculiar characteristics of his gospel?

20. Wherein does it differ from the other gospels?

21. What great doctrine does he unfold? John i. 1, 14, 34.

22. What doctrine in relation to man is brought out? John iii. 3, 5.

23. What beautiful and condensed gospel does he record? John iii. 16.

24. What precious address does he give, that is not given by the other evangelists? John xiv. etc.

25. What wonderful prayer of Jesus has he recorded? John xvii.

26. How were these evangelists able to report so accurately the words of Jesus, years after they were uttered? John xiv. 26.

27. Why should you carefully study this gospel of St. John? *Ans.* Because it presents the inner life of Jesus, the conditions of salvation, and the wonders and glories of redemption.

28. What does this inspired writer unfold in his first epistle? 1 John i. 1–3.

29. Why does the noble hero write? 1 John i. 4.

30. For what other reasons does he write? 1 John ii. 1, 12–14.

31. In what glorious language does he express his confidence and hopes? 1 John iii. 2.

32 What gives him the highest joy? 2 John 4; 3 John 3, 4

33. What revelation was made to him in the Isle of Patmos? Rev. i. 1.

34. How is the blessed Jesus revealed to him? Rev. i. 8.

35. What subjects are presented in this book of Revelation?

36. What splendid vision had he of heaven? Rev. xxi. 1, etc.

37. What precious invitation goes forth from this wonderful book? * Rev. xxii. 17.

* It is impossible for me to express, in language, my great admiration for the writings of this gifted and holy apostle, and I regret that my limits only allow me to point to a few stars, in the glorious constellation of truths, that shine upon us from his inspired intellect.

LESSON XLIX.

ST. STEPHEN, THE FIRST CHRISTIAN MARTYR.

1. What gave rise to the election of deacons in the Christian church? Acts vi. 1.

2. Who were these Grecians?

3. What did the twelve apostles say to the disciples? Acts vi. 2.

4. What did they tell the brethren to do? Acts vi. 3.

5. To what did they purpose to give themselves? Acts vi. 4.

6. Who were chosen to fill the office of deacon? Acts vi. 5.

7. What was the character of Stephen? Acts vi. 8.

8. Who disputed with him? Acts vi. 9.
9. What success did these disputants meet with? Acts vi. 10.
10. What promise was fulfilled in the case of Stephen? Luke xxi. 15.
11. Against whom were these Jews fighting? Acts v. 39.
12. To what did the opponents of Stephen next resort? Acts vi. 11.
13. What is meant by "they suborned men"?
14. What was the penalty, under the Jewish law, for blasphemy? Lev. xxiv. 14; 1 Kings xxi. 10.
15. Was this charge against Stephen true or false?
16. What was then done to Stephen? Acts vi. 12.
17. Who composed this "council"?
18. What other charges were brought against him? Acts vi. 13, 14.
19. How did God set his seal upon this holy man? Acts vi. 15.
20. What do you understand by "his face as it had been the face of an angel"?
21. What defence did Stephen make? Acts vii. 2, etc.
22. What bold charges did Stephen bring against his persecutors? Acts vii. 51–53.
23. How did they receive the truth from the lips of God's servant? Acts vii. 54.
24. Was Stephen alarmed by their rage?
25. What did he see, looking up? Acts vii. 55.
26. What did he say? Acts vii. 56.
27. What effect had this upon the people? Acts vii. 57.
28. What did they then do? Acts vii. 58.
29. What did Stephen say while being stoned? Acts vii. 59.
30. Whose example did he follow in this? Luke xxiii. 46.

31. What prayer did he offer for his persecutors? Acts vii. 60.
32. Whom did he imitate in this prayer? Luke xxiii. 34.
33. Who buried this holy martyr? Acts viii. 2.
34. What were some of the fruits of this martyrdom? Acts xi. 19–21.
35. Can you prove that the blood of the martyrs is the seed of the church?

LESSON L.

ST. JAMES, THE FIRST APOSTOLIC MARTYR.

1. How many prominent disciples of Jesus were there, by the name of James? Luke vi. 14, 15; Gal. i. 19.
2. Who is properly called James the First? Matt. iv. 21.
3. Who is James the Second? Matt. x. 3.
4. How is he distinguished from James the First? Mark xv. 40.
5. Who were his brethren? Matt. xxvii. 56; Luke vi. 16.
6. Who was the James spoken of in Acts xv. 13? *Ans.* Some suppose that he was the brother of Christ, and others that he was James, the son of Alpheus.
7. What does Josephus say of him? *Ans.* He is called by Josephus James the Just, and is said to have been stoned to death A. D. 62.
8. To whom is the general epistle of James ascribed? *Ans.* By some writers to James, the Lord's brother, by others to James the Less, and by some to James the First.

9. What is the general opinion? *Ans.* It is generally supposed to have been written by James the Just, about A. D. 61, shortly before his death?

10. What were James the First and his brother John called? Mark iii. 17.

11. Why were they called "sons of thunder"?

12. What did they want to do to the Samaritans, who would not receive Jesus? Luke ix. 54.

13. What did Jesus say to them? Luke ix. 55, 56.

14. What did the mother of these sons desire for them? Matt. xx. 20, 21.

15. What did Jesus say to her? Matt. xx. 22, 23.

16. Was James an intimate friend of his Master? Mark i. 28–31; v. 37.

17. Did he witness the miracles of Jesus? Mark i. 32–34.

18. Had he power to work miracles? Matt. x. 8.

19. With whom was he often associated? Matt. xvii. 1; Mark xiii. 3.

20. What did he witness on the mountain? Matt. xvii. 2–5.

21. How was James affected by the splendors of the scene? Matt. xvii. 6.

22. What did Jesus say to him and his companions? Matt. xvii. 7–9.

23. What questions did he put to Jesus privately? Mark xiii. 1–4.

24. What reply did Jesus make? Mark xiii. 5–8.

25. What warnings did he utter? Mark xiii. 9–12.

26. What promise was made? Mark xiii. 13.

27. On what solemn occasion did Christ take James with him? Mark xiv. 32–36.

28. What charge did he give to James and the other apostles? Mark xiv. 38.

29. What other scene did James witness? Mark xiv. 43–45.

30. What glorious scene did he behold? Mark xvi. 19.

31. By whom was this apostle put to death? Acts xii. 1, 2.
32. What year was this?
33. What can you say of the character of James, the first apostolic martyr?

LESSON LI.

ST. PAUL, THE FIRST MISSIONARY TO THE GENTILES.

1. Give some account of St Paul's early history. Acts xxii. 3.
2. How did he at first treat the Christians? Acts viii. 3.
3. Give an account of his conversion. Acts ix. 1–6.
4. What directions were given to Ananias? Acts ix. 10–16.
5. What was the result of his interview with Saul? Acts ix. 17, 18.
6. What did Saul then do? Acts ix. 20.
7. Did he now suffer persecution? Acts ix. 23, 24.
8. How did he escape? Acts ix. 25.
9. How did the other apostles receive him? Acts ix. 26–28.
10. Give some account of the sending forth of Paul and Barnabas to the Gentiles. Acts xiii. 1–3.
11. Whither did they go? Acts xiii. 4, 5, 13.
12. What other city did they visit? Acts xiii. 14.
13. What did Paul do in Antioch? Acts xiii. 16, etc.
14. How was his preaching received? Acts xiii. 42, 43.
15. What encouragement did Paul receive? Acts xiii. 44–49.

16. In what other places did they labor? Acts xiv. 1-7.

17. What miracle was performed here? Acts xiv. 8-10.

18. What was the effect upon the people? Acts xiv. 11-18.

19. What did they do next? Acts xiv. 19.

20. Did the noble apostle continue his labors? Acts xiv. 20-28.

21. What other missionary tour was undertaken? Acts xv. 36-41.

22. How is Paul led into Macedonia? Acts xvi. 9-13.

23. What occurred at Philippi? Acts xvi. 14-24.

24. How were Paul and Silas released from prison? Acts xvi. 25-27.

25. Who were converted that night? Acts xvi. 28-32.

26. What did the converts do? Acts xvi. 33, 34.

27. Under what circumstances did Paul and Silas leave the city? Acts xvi. 35-40.

28. Describe Paul's visit to Athens. Acts xvii. 16-34.

29. What other cities did he visit? Acts xviii. 1, 19, 23; xix. 1.

30. What countries did he afterward visit? Acts xx. 1, etc.

31. Describe his journey to Rome. Acts xxvi. 32; xxvii. 1, etc.

32. How long was he at Rome? Acts xxviii. 30.

33. Give an account of the death of St. Paul.

LESSON LII.

ST. PAUL, THE HEROIC APOSTLE OF JESUS CHRIST.

1. Where do you find the character of St. Paul fully brought out?
2. How many of his epistles have we in the New Testament?
3. Which are they?
4. Why were they written?
5. What do they bring out besides the character of their author?
6. At what period were they written?
7. What can you say of their style?
8. What does St. Paul call himself in these epistles? Rom. i. 1.
9. With what salutation does he greet those to whom he writes? Rom. i. 7; 1 Cor. i. 2; Gal. i. 3; Eph. i. 2; Phil. i. 2, etc.
10. For what does he render thanks to God? Rom. i. 8; 1 Cor. i. 4; Phil. i. 3; Col. i. 3, 4.
11. What proof is there that St. Paul was a man of earnest prayer? Rom. i. 9; 1 Thess. iii. 10; Phil. i. 4; Col. i. 9.
12. How does he show his interest in the spiritual good of all men? Rom. i. 14–16.
13. What is he willing to do for others? 2 Cor. xii. 14, 15.
14. How does he show his sincerity? 2 Cor. iv. 1–2.
15. How does he manifest his firmness of character? 2 Cor. iv. 8, 9.
16. What inspired him with the power of endurance? 2 Cor. iv. 17; Rom. viii. 18.
17. **What fired his zeal? 2 Cor. v. 13–15.**

18. Did St. Paul greatly enjoy his work? 2 Cor. i. 4; vii. 4; Phil. ii. 17.

19. How did he view tribulations? Rom. v. 3–5.

20. What account does he give of his persecutions and trials? 2 Cor. xi. 24–27.

21. What views did he have of the heavenly state? 2 Cor. xii. 1–4.

22. What influence had these revelations upon him? 2 Cor. v. 1–4; Phil. i. 23.

23. To what work did he confine himself? 1 Cor. ii. 2.

24. In what did he glory? Gal. vi. 14.

25. How did he value the knowledge of Christ? Phil. iii. 8.

26. How does he show his modesty? 1 Cor. ii. 1, 4, 5.

27. To whom does he give all the glory of his work? 1 Cor. iii. 6, 7.

28. What is the great desire of his heart in relation to others? Eph. iii. 16–19.

29. What ascription leaps from his soul? Eph. iii. 20, 21.

30. What does the noble hero write to Timothy? 2 Tim. iv. 6.

31. When and where was this written?

32. What had the Christian warrior fought? 2 Tim. iv. 7.

33. What was laid up for him? 2 Tim. iv. 8.

34. Will you give your views of the life, character, trials, and achievements of St. Paul?

35. Will you adopt his sublime aim as yours? Phil. iii. 13, 14.

36. Will you accept, in conclusion, this benediction? Heb. xiii. 20, 21.

www.ingramcontent.com/pod-product-compliance
Lightning Source LLC
LaVergne TN
LVHW011120110826
845150LV00008B/2192
* 9 7 8 1 4 2 5 5 0 6 8 8 9 *